FIREBALL

FIREBALL

*If I looked as good
as Fireball, I would
drive a STOCK CAR, TOO!
Bald, chubby guys are
NOT Allowed To race, only
write Books! Enjoy!*

by GODWIN KELLY

[an unauthorized biography]

CARBON
PRESS

Dedication

To my family –
Diane, Ellie, Casey and Kahlin –
for providing the love and patience
necessary to see this project to completion.

First published in 2005 by Carbon Press, LC
520 Ridgewood Ave, Daytona Beach, FL 32117 USA
386.947.1986   fax 208.441.8336
www.CarbonPressOnline.com

The information in this book is true and
complete to the best of our knowledge.

We recognize that some words, model names and designations,
for example, mentioned herein are the property of the trademark holder.
We use them for identification purposes only. This is not an official publication.

Carbon Press books may be purchased for educational, business or
sales-promotional use. For details write or call Carbon Press.

ISBN: 0-9724378-5-1

Designed by Wade Caldwell

Printed in the United States
First Edition (Second Printing)

Table of Contents

Special Acknowledgements

SPECIAL THANKS TO:

Judy Judge	Richard Childress
Max Muhleman	Ray Evernham
Ned Jarrett	Rusty Wallace
H.A. "Humpy" Wheeler	Chuck Warren
Deb Williams	Mel Larson
Dave Markowitz	Paul Sawyer
JoAnne Roberts	Rev. Hal Marchman
David Poole	Johnny Rutherford
Josh Davidson	Richard Petty
Bobby Allison	Leonard Wood
Chris Economaki	Buz McKim
Dick Dolan	Curtis "Crawfish" Crider
Junior Johnson	Greg Fielden
Leo Mehl	Bob Snodgrass
Ray Fox	Dick Thompson
Irwin "Speedy" Spiers	Jeanne Barnes
Bob Laney	Bob Moore
Tim Sullivan	Ken Willis
Bob Meyers	D.C. Williams Jr.
Bill Gazaway	Marvin Panch

Special thanks to Mars, Inc., for making M&Ms with peanuts and Dunkin' Donuts for their late-night, drive-through latte service. Successful conclusion could not have been achieved without their sugar and caffeine-saturated products.

Introduction

January 20, 2005

His name was Edward Glenn Roberts, Jr., but to millions of race fans, he was simply known as "Fireball." The name Fireball Roberts lingers in the air around racetracks like a perfume aroma in a ballroom, yet few of today's contemporary drivers know much about the legend, let alone his secret and tragic love affair.

During a late night telephone conversation in June, 2004 with driver Rusty Wallace, I lobbed this question at him – what can you tell me about Fireball Roberts?

"I'm absolutely familiar with the name, but that was before my time," Wallace said. "I don't know anything about his personality. It's a cool first name. I don't know anything about him, like I should. He's an icon."

I cornered car owner Ray Evernham in the garage at Darlington (S.C.) Raceway in November and asked him the same question.

"I know he was one of NASCAR's top stock car drivers. I know he was burned critically in a fire at Charlotte," he said. "He's a part of our history and someone that when you come into the sport, you just automatically got to have respect for."

Richard Childress, who fields three Nextel Cup cars and was car owner to Dale Earnhardt for almost two decades, watched Roberts race at short tracks in North Carolina when he was a kid. "He definitely had his own style and that's what made him special," Childress said. "He was one of the pioneers that was changing the sport back then and probably didn't realize it."

Bingo!

Bobby Allison made his first Nextel Cup (then Grand National) start in 1961 when Roberts was in his prime. "He certainly added some class to an early part of this industry that started down there in the grass, you know what I mean, out there in the dirt," Allison said. "He was one of the ones that really did good things for the sport in his career."

Fireball Roberts, the racer, had quite a career, winning 33 races from 1950 until 1964. He is considered the best driver never to win the NASCAR championship (although, you'll get a strong and viable argument from Junior Johnson on the subject).

The people who helped build what NASCAR is today, men like Fireball, are largely forgotten in modern times. I talked to Bill Gazaway, the former Nextel Cup Series director, on the subject.

"No, they don't," said Gazaway on people remembering old-time racers and their vast contributions. "He was from a different era. There's very few of those people today that know people from the old era, you know, from the earlier times."

That is a funny trait about stock car racing. While former players from baseball and football are revered, it seems racing forgets its greats. "You got to remember that back then, the media wrote about Lou Gehrig, Babe Ruth, Joe DiMaggio and people like that. Motorsports was nothing. You don't know what a problem we had even to just get an ad in the paper. So, naturally people wouldn't remember."

What truly makes the Fireball Roberts story intriguing were the twists and turns of his personal life, the story behind the story of this great asphalt athlete; a story that has never fully been told.

When a biographical search for Fireball Roberts at www.amazon.com turned up "no results," I appointed myself to fill the void and tell the tale of this man of swagger, passion and great abilities as a driver, and, a lover. I found out that trying to capture a man's life in print is like stuffing a rhino into a shoebox – it doesn't happen easily.

It is my hope this won't be the last book written about this mysterious master of fast machines. There are several others among us who personally knew Fireball Roberts and I hope, someday, they come forward with their stories of this amazing individual; a man who reshaped the very perimeters of racing, who may have actually saved a sport flailing in the troubled waters of the late 1950s. May this be the first volume of many more to follow.

Anyone who loves stock car racing owes Fireball Roberts a giant debt of gratitude for his accomplishments and courage.

– Godwin Kelly

In Memory of Deborah and Roger

Foreword

January 18, 2005

It must have been sometime in 1958 that I first met Glenn Roberts; met him in the sense of getting to know someone. As one of a very small group of southern sports writers who wrote about stock car racing in our daily newspapers at that time, I wasn't sure that adopting a new hero named "Fireball," who was about to join up with a crew chief/car owner named "Smokey," was going to raise my stock much in the news room of "The *Charlotte News*," my employer. As at most dailies then, even in the south, there was still some question that these racers might be more closely related to "rasslers" than to college hoops, much less a bona fide big time sport like major league baseball.

Absolutely no one called Glenn Roberts, Jr., anything but Fireball in those days, whether in print or in the pits. The special exception, as Godwin Kelly's fine work makes clear herein, was the sweet love of his life, Judy Judge, whose courageous and loyal life is itself worthy of a book. Of course, his immediate family didn't count. Maybe a few of his pals in Florida who knew him longest also used his real name, but I would bet that they, too, caved in to the magical resonance of Fireball, a nickname destined for immortality in the pantheon of all-time best sports hero sobriquets.

As our friendship grew over the next several years, I would sneak in a "Glenn" once in a while myself. But I couldn't help reverting to Fireball as the right name for the man who had the look, the physique, and of course the talent and bravery, to drive the very life out of the rip-snorting, thunderous, magnificent-looking black and gold #22 Pontiacs that Smokey Yunick would give him; the world's best bull breeder, challenging the finest matador on the planet.

At this point in time, some 40 years and two generations since Fireball died of his burns at Charlotte Memorial Hospital, fans seem fascinated by his legacy. Certainly there are many millions more following the sport now than then, and the fan base is now truly national,

San Diego to Bangor, Seattle to Key West. Invariably this leads to the assessment and question, "That Fireball Roberts must have been really something. Wonder what it was that made him stand out so much back then?" Godwin Kelly has done the best job I've seen yet of piecing together the answer in this excellent biography/narrative. Two quotes which Godwin got, one from Fred Lorenzen, the other from Smokey Yunick, jumped out at me as especially incisive and telling answers to that perennial question above. Lorenzen, who was really something special himself, said, "He was the best…He was brains and throttle in a league by himself"—a superb synopsis of how Fireball could be so consistently fast and win so much, despite the mechanical and tire demons of that time. Smokey, the most quotable—and perhaps the smartest—man the sport had seen, said, in his earthy style, "Fireball had the skill and the balls, and he was the smartest of the drivers…His plan was simple: sit on the pole and lead every lap…If Fireball had a tire that could have stood up under the punishment he put on them, his record would be something that would never have been equaled…He was the original hero of the superspeedways."

Finally, I'm personally glad that Godwin devoted so much emphasis and detail to the incredible season of 1962. It was the peak, and, as Judy Judge shares with us, it was the beginning of the end—the year Fireball started making plans to quit driving, marry her and transition into a spokesman career.

1962…I can see him now, bursting into sight way down in the fourth turn at Daytona—or is it Darlington?…the sun creating hot spots of reflection off the gold leaf Smokey used to paint the bold "22" on the doors and roof, the whole car moving with a power and suddenness that only it generated…Your heartbeat accelerated as you saw he had swept by the previous leader and was going faster, faster, faster than anything else on the track…Here he comes, that mighty engine in full song, making the deepest, loudest noise of all—WHOOSH!—and there he goes, in a glorious storm of power, daring and mastery…disappearing, but leaving an unforgettable image burned into our memory.

– Max Muhleman

FIREBALL

Head Over Heels

These two were hopelessly in love.

On this night, like a thousand before it, they looked into each other's eyes and exchanged their most intimate feelings for each other.

Edward Glenn Roberts, Jr. was a strapping and ruddy 35-year-old best described as a real man, who cast a great shadow over his little universe.

Roberts, who went by his middle name, stood a towering 6-foot-2 and sported, large muscular arms; forearms that looked like they could pulverize steel. He sported a neat crew cut and had been blessed with a captivating smile and a deep, hearty laugh.

Oh man, that laugh.

Glenn would make a joke and those vigorous laughs, the kind that radiate up from the belly, would cause his head to kick back so far all you could see was chin and Adam's apple.

His face was wide and chiseled from granite, his eyes held straight by deep running crow's feet, the end result from years of excessive

chortling, no doubt, and long playful days at the beach.

Those blue eyes – bright and alive – are where Judy could measure his emotional state at any given moment in time. They became fiery and wild and danced when he was angry. They shined when he was happy. They could make Judy's knees rattle and her tummy turn to jelly when the lights went down low.

Judy, a tiny package of adorable, will tell you Glenn was extremely fussy about his appearance. The pants had to be pressed; his shirts wrinkle free; his shoes had to gloss or they stayed in the closet.

The man was impeccable, a poster boy for spit shine.

Glenn had some money in the bank and mighty big plans for his future which included the love of his life, who was a daughter of a local, hard-nosed, whiskey-drinking judge.

Glenn and Judy were raised in the same speck-on-the-map resort town nestled on Florida's sleepy east coast, but lived in vastly different worlds.

When they first met, Glenn was 29 and by that time could be easily classified as "worldly" thanks to his rugged looks, disarming charm, overwhelming charisma and extensive travels.

It was no secret that Glenn Roberts was the consummate lady's man, a guy who would have women knock at his motel door wearing nothing but a raincoat hoping to spark an invite for a frolicking night of high-octane lovemaking.

He had been from one end of the country to the other utilizing a talent few humans truly possess – he could flat drive the beejezus out of a race car, taking thousands of spectators for the thrill of their lives with his skill and derring-do.

So, you take his good looks, toss in two heaping cups of charisma, sprinkle in unfathomable bravado behind the wheel of a souped-up hot rod and women, it seems, were left somewhat powerless, eager to tap this love-making machine during his roaring 20s.

There was an interesting twist. Glenn's wife, yes wife, Doris Roberts, didn't seem to mind, or at the very least, she quietly tolerated this man of unbridled passion, who conquered not only stock car racing, but the fancy of young females all across this great nation.

E. Glenn Roberts Jr. lived the ultimate double life during most of his adulthood. To outsiders he was a happy family man with an admiring daughter. To racing insiders he was a disarming rogue with an unquenchable thirst for speedway glory, fun and females.

Glenn's approach to life started to change when Judy arrived on the scene. Judy was 20, going to Stetson University in nearby DeLand, and protected by a demanding father. She was raised with high moral values but was very spirited. She looked at life through big, brown doe eyes. Men, who didn't meet the standards of high society, seemingly had no chance with this dazzling woman. Even one of Roberts' best friends, Bob Laney, told him to forget about it; she was "unattainable."

That first meeting occurred in their hometown of Daytona Beach, Fla., at a nightclub called the Martinique, a hangout for young people off Main Street on the beachside. He introduced himself that night as Bobby Edwards and said he was an engineer. From that starting point, they slowly built a

relationship – much like two players in a fencing duel maneuvering for position during a match.

Spin! Advance! Thrust!

Retreat and repeat.

Touché!

Judy did not discover Glenn's true identity until she spotted his picture in the 1959 Daytona 500 program while attending her first race at Daytona International Speedway. She had been invited to a race by another male friend. It was the Saturday afternoon before the inaugural 500 and the track was hosting a companion event. Needless to say, Judy was startled and mad. Maybe pissed is a better description. After she saw his photo, her outrage carried her straight to the garage area. They talked through a chain-link fence.

"Well, hello Fireball!" Judy said, adding later, "I think that was the only time I ever called him Fireball."

"We really need to talk," Glenn said, hat in hand.

They met back at the Martinique that night, the night before the Daytona 500, and Bobby Edwards, err, Glenn Roberts, explained himself.

"We talked, we danced, then he told me that he was afraid to tell me who he was because he was afraid I wouldn't have anything to do with him," she said. "I told him 'You are right. I wouldn't have.' "

Then he told me, "You mean a lot to me. I hope this doesn't change anything."

It didn't.

Judy was interested in a long-term relationship and she saw promise in this racetrack man. She wanted no part of a sexual fling with the life span of a bottle rocket flight. So, they continued to date for another five months before the mega bombshell fell on her life. On July 5, 1959, she found out he was married (store that date in your memory). He certainly didn't play the part of a married man, since he was out on the town seemingly every night. There was absolutely nothing domestic about Glenn Roberts. "We'd go make the scene," Bob Laney said. "He was pretty much out six nights a week."

The day after winning the 1959 Firecracker 250 at Daytona's new speedway, Mr. Judge confronted Glenn at Stephens Pontiac, his sponsor, where he was appearing with his winning stock car.

"My father showed up and asked him if he was having an affair with me," Judy says. "I didn't know that all this was going on because I was at school in DeLand. Glenn told my dad, 'No, I'm not having an affair with her, I love her.' Doris had called Daddy. Doris said someone had seen us out, so she called Daddy to tell him.

"After their (Glenn-Mr. Judge) conversation was finished at the car dealership, which wasn't pleasant at all, Glenn came to DeLand to tell me. Daddy told me I had to choose between Glenn and the family. I chose Glenn, because at that point, there was no family for me."

What a gamble for the strong-minded sprite from a prim and proper family. She had been groomed her whole life to be a proper lady and now she was cavorting with a hell-raising race car driver.

Looking well beyond Glenn's playboy veneer, she saw many rock solid traits such as honesty (well, he got a lot better), dependability and sensitivity. Oh yeah, he was good looking, damn good looking, and funny as hell, and had money and name recognition.

They soon became an item, and the town gossips had a field day. After the initial shock wore off, Judy and Glenn didn't care. They were in love, blind love, the kind that makes all around you a blur. How did Judy know she was "the one?" Glenn started to insist she travel with him to all his racing events.

"If you don't come along with me, I'm gonna get laid," he told her. "It's just human nature." Soon, they were sharing an apartment, they affectionately called "the pad." A few years later, Glenn rewarded Judy with her own house, their own little love palace. "This is my first home," he said to her.

Glenn was once, and for all, spoken for, oh, except for that little matter of exchanging wedding vows with the former Doris McConnell before a York, South Carlina judge about nine years earlier.

This whole situation was as prickly as a sand spur, magnified by the fact they lived in Daytona Beach, a very small, close-knit vacation village in the 1950s and early '60s, and Glenn was a recognizable sports figure, and Judy was the child of a tough-nosed, trial-tested, no-nonsense father.

Oh, yes, and Doris. Years earlier, she had given up on Glenn's  endless philandering and appetite for one-night stands. Then this homegrown girl, the willowy Judy Judge, showed up one day and messed up their whole dysfunctional but cozy relationship. She was a real threat. Judy had captured the heart of Glenn, and Doris was not going to let go of her prize without a Godzilla-sized fight.

Lord, what a mess.

Despite the whispers around town, they clung to each other like the grapevine hugs a post. They created their own world and forged ahead with their relationship with the promise of brighter days ahead.

Friends say they became inseparable. They went out to dinner, frolicked on the beach, drank at bars all over town, laughed with friends and traveled to racetracks from Georgia to Southern California.

It was one hell of a ride and Judy expected it to get even better. Roberts and his wife were officially divorced on April 15, 1964. The papers were filed in St. Johns County, two counties up the coast from Daytona. According to friends of the family, Doris Roberts didn't want to publicize the split because of the stigma in those days of losing hold of a husband.

Getting the divide from Doris was Step 1 for Glenn. Step 2 was to finish up his racing obligations with Ford, then along the way accomplish Step 3 – marrying Judy. NASCAR president Bill France, Sr. suggested Glenn and Judy marry in the infield of Daytona International Speedway the morning of the Firecracker 400. Judy said France told them, "It would be good publicity." The thought of track nuptials was appalling to Glenn and Judy; they set their wedding date for June 6. The plan was for him to retire as a race car driver and become a spokesman for a beer company. He had already signed a deal; a big, juicy, fat contract.

Judy could not wait for all this to happen. She had lived her life in the shadows as "the other woman" for several years and was ready to march Glenn to the chapel and start enjoying their new life together. She wanted a proper wedding. She wanted her daddy to walk her down the aisle. She wanted to have the full blown matrimony experience and not elope. Glenn felt the same way. Glenn had done that once before and the marriage vows apparently didn't take root.

The very best part of their relationship was when they were alone. Judy and Glenn would melt into each others arms at night. He would tell her things that no other ears on the planet would ever hear. It was wonderful, Judy now says, with a sigh.

Then came May 24, 1964.

On that particular night, they were once again alone and tenderly whispering to each other. But this time, the scene was much different. Fireball Roberts, the famed stock car driver, was fighting to stay alive.

"They brought him from the emergency room and his face looked sunburned," Judy said 40 years later, remembering the horror of the situation as if it happened yesterday.

"His shoulders looked untouched. They had the sheet up to his shoulders. I leaned over and kissed him and he said, 'I'm gonna be sore as hell tomorrow.' "

When Judy first arrived at Charlotte's Memorial Hospital, the news was nothing less than grim.

"The doctor took me aside and told me, 'I don't think he's gonna live,' " she said.

Glenn Roberts was not going to let that happen, not that night, and instructed his young fiancée` "Don't let me go to sleep."

"They put him on his tummy on his bed," Judy said. "I sat on the floor under his face and talked to him all that night."

And so began the beginning of a horrible end.

1950
9 Starts, 1 Pole
3 Races Led
1,138 Laps, 60 Laps Led
1 Win, Rank: 2
Winnings: $6,800

Every Night But Saturday Night

Race car drivers, oh man, now there is an interesting study in abnormal behavior.

Some think they are foolhardy souls while others believe this breed of human being is born without fear. How about just plain dumb? This peculiar Homo sapien's offshoot is generally male, and like the lion, enjoys having several females in the surrounding area. Grrrrrrrr.

The true racer is of rare blood, unwittingly motivated by primitive instinct, the raw emotion, the excitement of competition. Some of the best racers in history have utilized the least amount of language, preferring to let their skills behind the wheel do the talking. They honk and howl like primates in the jungle.

Stock car racing has long been a breeding ground for these lovable, modern-day, helmet-toting troglodytes. When eavesdropping on a conversation, say between a race car driver and his chief mechanic, you will likely hear a driver respond with one syllable answers like "yep" and "tires" and "wedge" and "fuck."

It's completely guttural, halfway savage.

When you mix among this tribe, hear the language spoken, the garage area at a racetrack begins to look more like a series of adjoining caves. Take a deep breath and inhale the smell of exhaust, rubber, oil and gasoline. Close your eyes and exhale. You can sense the hairy testosterone in the air all around you. This is man holding a large dinosaur bone vs. man wielding a stalagmite fragment. This is ultimate macho.

Yes, stock car racing is a man's world: make that a manly man's world. Who the hell else would strap their bodies tight against a 3,400-pound metal beast with enough horsepower to reach speeds of 200 miles per hour and zip through turns banked as high as a three story building?

Christ, almighty.

Not only are these men traveling at a blinding clip, but they are joined by 40 or so other guys on the track trying to claw their way to the front of this speed pack in search of a trophy, fame, glory and recognition among their peers.

What makes a man do this?

In most cases money is secondary to the plain thrill of balls-out competition. As a driver becomes older and wiser but mostly older, then yes, the money does become much more important. If you count endorsements, today's top drivers gross as much or more than a pro football or baseball player.

How much? Well, we are talking about paychecks that total in the millions of dollars as major league stock car racing reaches new audiences and taps corporate America's vault of sponsorship dollars.

The "NASCAR Nation" is all the rage, but racing is hardly a new phenomenon. Competition among men in cars has been around, well, since the horseless carriage first arrived in the late 19th and early 20th centuries.

They were racing in Europe before 1900 and in America soon after.

One of the first races staged on U.S. soil was actually held on hard-packed sand near Daytona Beach. Two guys in two cars raced side-by-side just north of Daytona on the beach in 1903.

Those two gentlemen were not racing for money that day; they were fishtailing through sand to see who had the fastest equipment, giving little or no concern to their personal well-being or the ill effects of an unexpected accident. Sandpipers and turtles and slow-moving elderly beware.

They were racing, damn it. That is what this game is all about.

Men. Machines. Speed. Competition. Courage. Gas. Smoke. Oil. Rubber.

And on the second floor of the driver psyche during the 1950s and '60s: booze, partying and women, lots of women. And more booze. And more women. Racing is an aphrodisiac, both for those in the cars, and those behind the catch fence.

If the other guy was fast, you must go faster and be more furious. It's not the thrill of the chase. You see, the chase is the thrill. Winning the chase is pure ecstasy, better than a

DAYTONA WINNER: Glenn "Fireball" Roberts, seated in white uniform, rests after being presented trophy for "Daytona Firecracker 250" victory July 4 from Miss Patti Pennington as Chief Mechanic Banjo Matthews looks on from right. Matthews led the race for 61 laps. Both Matthews and Roberts were driving 1962 Pontiacs and both are already looking forward to the fifth annual "Daytona 500" Feb. 24, 1963.

long bath, eating a box of velvet chocolates or sipping a $500 bottle of champagne.

Winning a stock car racing event brings about toe-clenching, fist-pumping exhilaration, an adrenalin rush so fierce that at that very moment of triumph, the victor generally screams out in uncontrollable delight.

"Oh yeah! Yeah baby! We did it!"

Then, there's the dark side of the sport. Drivers have always given little thought to the potential consequences of their actions or to the physics of a stock car striking an unforgiving concrete wall at excessive speed.

If they really thought about it, they could not drive a race car, because they would be too concerned about injury and unable to function. Drivers, such as the great Fireball Roberts, raced with reckless abandon, storing danger issues in a brown box, hidden deep in their mental pantry.

Safety measures usually advance in leaps and bounds when a leader of the racing sect is struck down in action. Most recently Dale Earnhardt, thought to be invincible by his peers, died on the last lap of the 2001 Daytona 500 at Daytona International Speedway. Earnhardt, a seven-time national champion, died instantly from massive head and neck injuries after his stock car slammed the concrete wall in Turn 4. In response to the horrifying accident, the sanctioning body commissioned exhaustive studies, new safety equipment was developed and rules were implemented to protect drivers from the same grisly fate.

No matter what safety initiatives are taken, racing will be a very dangerous game with no guarantees any driver will be 100 percent safe from death or severe injury.

Speed kills.

While racing has always been hazardous, the early 1960s were especially brutal because car makers had developed high-powered engines, which produced ungodly speed, but failed to meet the same technology levels with other aspects of the cars.

"It was a dangerous time," said Leo Mehl, who worked as an engineer with Goodyear Tires, then ran the division for nearly two decades. "In 1964 two drivers were killed just doing tire tests."

"You think about that period of time, and, well, imagine a tire company killing two guys in tire testing today and staying in racing more than 24 hours? Tires were a big issue then. They were basically running modified passenger tires. It was an unbelievably dangerous era."

The tires used in those days were asked to over-achieve race after race on stock car racing's biggest and fastest tracks. Braking systems were primitive. Seat belt harness systems were crude.

Race teams welded extra metal pieces, mostly metal pipe, into the cockpit which was called a "roll cage." This was done to keep the roof and sides of the car from crushing in on the driver if the car made impact with other cars, walls, guard rails and dirt barriers.

Drivers wore a helmet and used lap belts and/or shoulder harnesses to keep them from ejecting from the car during an accident.

In the old, old, old days of racing, drivers did not use seat belts believing it was better to separate from the car in an accident than stay along for the whole ride. Now come on, you have to admit that is crazy, but old-school masculine.

Stock car racing reached a new level of lethal in the early 1960s as more high-banked superspeedways (paved ovals more than a mile long) sprouted up like ragweed in the South.

The cars were going really fast but did not offer the driver adequate protection. These racetracks, which quickly became fan favorites, offered a real examination of driver mettle and tested their ability to stow the unpleasant mental images of crashing at a high rate of speed.

"When I look back on these guys that survived that era, and

are still involved with the sport, the fact they are still alive is a huge accomplishment," Mehl said. "There was a lot of gallows humor among drivers and all kinds of crazy stuff would go on because it was so dangerous. They would do things (party) because it was a release.

"I don't want to be maudlin about it, but I think the era that these guys lived and survived, shows a passion for doing something that doesn't and can't exist today because nobody can understand how dangerous it was in those days."

Chris Economaki, the editor and publisher emeritus of *National Speed Sport News* and the dean of all racing journalists, said danger and death sold tickets in those days. "I was at Watkins Glen (N.Y.) for a Formula One race and a guy went under the guard rail and was decapitated," Economaki said. "A couple of guys in the pits said, 'Well, we needed that to keep the danger element alive in this sport.' It was terrible to have that kind of opinion. Some people looked at it like that."

Those who triumphed at the new cathedrals of speed and escaped the cold grip of death became heroes. Those who died were mourned and for the most part, quickly forgotten, because it was an accepted part of the game, a very gruesome part of the game.

Race car drivers don't expend much energy or thought on the aspects of death. They have a tendency to simply ignore it. They steer clear of negative issues. Drivers don't participate in this sport at gunpoint. Any man who has ever participated on a racetrack willingly grabbed the steering wheel with both hands and smashed the gas pedal with his right foot believing he would survive the day. To this day professional drivers carry that mindset in addition to millions of dollars in disability and life insurance coverage.

In order to maintain mental balance, they must tell themselves a little lie race after race after race – "It won't be me today." The lure of competition, the tug of unbridled speed glory outweighs the chance of death or becoming an invalid.

Forty or so years back, many of these men would ease their fears with a nightly ritual of a woman in one hand and a cold, alcohol beverage in the other. If they survived the day, many would celebrate the night. It was a curious cycle.

"There were a lot of bad things happening," says H.A. "Humpy" Wheeler, president of Lowe's Motor Speedway since 1975 and the racing version of P.T. Barnum.

"It was probably the worst period of time race-wise that we, and NASCAR, had ever been through. Indy cars were having problems, too. They were crashing and burning. In stock car racing, they were going from the old-timey racing at dirt tracks to the superspeedway era. As much as we thought we knew about superspeedways in those days, the fact was, nobody knew anything.

"A lot of good race car drivers Glenn raced against, could never make that transition from the short tracks to the superspeedways. People don't think race drivers get scared, but they do. These big tracks scared some people and they just didn't want to die. Some short track guys just couldn't take to the superspeedways. Fireball did.

"He came out of dirt racing and he was not the predominant driver down there. He became predominant on the superspeedways. Russ Catlin, probably racing's greatest publicist, named Fireball 'The Master of Asphalt' because he drove so well on asphalt."

The early 1960s was a trying time for these "asphaltnauts" who were pioneering a new and very dangerous form of race car driving. Wheeler thinks back to the design of those American-made, V8-powered sedans and shudders.

"(Racing) technology surpassed safety and that's what always brings a lot of lethal accidents," he said. "In those days it was paper-thin bodies on the cars that had huge blasphemous engines that just put out tons of horsepower and very narrow tires and of course no safety inner-liner…It was pretty apparent to everybody in racing that something drastically needed to be done."

Trying times for race car drivers? Not after the sun melted in the western horizon and the party started back at the designated motel room.

Before he fell in love with Judy Judge, Fireball Roberts was one of the ring leaders in this nightly circus. In his autobiography, legendary mechanic and inventor Smokey Yunick wrote, "We were duty bound to get drunk and entertain the ladies, (the pioneer women race fans). You lady race fans today owe a little gratitude to those lady race fans who stayed up to 5 a.m. partying with us, and having to go home, or to work with a terrible hangover and face their fathers, husbands and boyfriends. Every night but Saturday night was party night."

This was a wonderful, yet horrifying, time in stock car racing history, and the man leading the blistering charge down the track and sometimes back at the party, was E. Glenn Roberts Jr.

1951

9 Starts, 0 Poles
0 Races Led
825 Laps, 0 Laps Led
0 Wins, Rank: 12
Winnings: $1,685

The Heart of Charlotte

It was May 23, 1964, the night before the World 600 at Charlotte Motor Speedway, a gigantic speedway built due north of North Carolina's "Queen City." Now under Humpy Wheeler's long reign, the track is called Lowe's Motor Speedway, thanks to a multi-million dollar facility naming contract.

This course, which measures 1.5 miles long and has turns banked at 24 degrees, opened for business in 1960. The banking allowed the heavy, brutish automobiles of the day to run speeds comparable to those turned by purpose-built race cars at Indianapolis Motor Speedway.

That was the magic of stock car racing in those days. The era's top drivers traveled at break-neck speed in cars that looked much like the family sedan back home in the garage. The motto of manufacturers was: "Win on Sunday, sell on Monday." It was a strong lure that hooked many a blue collar working man in the Southeast.

At this stage of the sport's development, it was hard to find a true fan north of the Mason-Dixon Line or west of the mighty Mississippi.

This was primarily a Southern, summer pastime pumped with dollars from the national automotive industry. An average race at a small track would attract 8,000 to 10,000 folks. These big, new glistening stadiums would lure 40,000 to 50,000. There was no network television and only patchwork radio networks. The mainstream national media paid little or no attention to this provincial sports oddity. The stick-and-ball journalists of the time felt stock car racing was not a true sport and not worth their attention.

After all, NASCAR racing was an offshoot of the Bible Belt's moonshine trade, a shady, black-market business that put a premium on fast cars and quick-thinking drivers. The common perception of stock car racing was a bunch of dirty hillbillies and redneck hooligans racing like a bunch of idiots in full throttle circles with their hooch-carrying sedans.

Crazy-assed dopes, all of them.

Well, not all of them.

By 1964 the personality of the sport was changing. Some of the men in these fast machines did not have a Confederate pedigree. They hailed from California and Illinois and the Northeast and migrated knowing the only decent money in the sport of racing was being doled out in the Deep South.

Southern stock car racing may have had only a regional audience but it was still the big league, the final stop for young jockeys vying for a handful of elite driving positions. These drivers, many of them young and some good looking, all had a little cash in their back pockets, were constantly away from home and all the time attracting admiring females.

For the most part, society shunned racing types. Racers were shoved into the same classification as carnival people and gypsies. Almost everybody goes to the county fair or will get their fortunes told but few socialize with the hired help. Get the picture?

But these drivers were much different. Yes, they would float from town to town, but they had an exciting lifestyle. Imagine having a job where people paid money to cheer you on and you could perish at any given moment. Women seeking men with a bad-boy image would surround a racing motel like children mobbing the neighborhood ice cream man on a summer afternoon.

The late-night parties in those days were notorious, as young racers frolicked with women who were tantalized by their profession, much like a rock-and-roll band which attracts a gaggle of groupies after each performance.

"The younger they were, the better it was," said a racing mechanic of the day. "We would have T-shirt parties. That's all anyone could wear was a T-shirt." And there were the infamous "coat hanger parties."

One of the manufacturer reps of the day carried a bag full of mink covered coat hangers. "He'd pass them out to the girls, and say, 'You're invited to the party. Here's your coat hanger – to hang your clothes on.' They always had something going on."

The night before the 1964 World 600 there was no big party. It was different. Roberts wasn't in a giddy merrymaking mood that night. He was in good spirits, yet quiet and pensive as he held court poolside at the Heart of Charlotte motel.

Joe Whitlock, who knocked around racing as a motorsports journalist, PR man and back door marketing genius, wrote about that night 10 years later:

He was relaxed and talkative, stretched out in one of those plastic-ribbed poolside chairs with his feet propped up under a metal table. It could have been any of a thousand motels but it was the Heart of Charlotte.

He rippled a deck of cards, almost unconsciously, still grinning from a 75 cent gin rummy victory with Gene White, a close friend who had left to go to dinner. The muffled traffic noise from distant Tryon Street mingled with occasional burst of laughter from other groups around the pool. It was a warm sound. The hint of a breeze in the spring evening air made relaxing and talking easy.

Fireball Roberts was at peace with the world.

"Got a secret for this race," he said through a chuckle. "Sully (Jack Sullivan, the crew chief on Robert's No. 22 Ford) is gonna hang a wishbone on the sign over our pits. That oughta do it. Charlotte's the only big track I haven't won on. A little luck and that will change tomorrow."

This was taken Sunday May 17 – the day before we left for Charlotte. That is Tammy Wilson, daughter of Mary Ann + Jack – riding with Glenn, I love this picture! He was happy and we were having fun.

Roberts rolled his close-cropped head back, looking up at the stars, and rambling on. Talking to the sky. Just talking.

"Look at that sky. Makes me want to be down on the river with my dog… waiting for daylight and ducks. I used to think that retriever was dumb, but it was me and not the dog. He got so tired of me missing ducks last season, he started retrieving for the guy in the next blind. Wait 'till next season. Got a new gun and me and that dog are gonna get enough ducks to last all winter.

"Race drivers are a lot like retrievers. The good ones are. Got to be patient. When it's time to make a move you've got to move. Concentration and patience. That's what I'm doing with this Charlotte track. Taking my time. I'll have to win here sooner or later. It's just a matter of time."

On and on. Relaxing and talking about everything in general and nothing in particular. Hunting. Racing. Shooting pool. Flying.

Football. Winning. Cheating. Losing. Even renaming half the small towns in Texas.

From time to time another driver or mechanic, or just a fan, would stop by for a quick chat and a "good luck in tomorrow's race."

"Oh, we'll get 'em," Roberts would say. "I'm ready.

RECORDS, ROBERTS, RACING,
that's the Rebel 300

The eighth annual Rebel 300 last May 9, like its predecessors made news and history from the first day of practice, five days before the race.

Practice speeds were high; in fact, not a single stable slowed work until their charges were cruising steadily above the track record. That fell on Monday by two miles an hour when no less than nine drivers erased the old mark. Fast Freddy Lorenzen, for the fourth year in a row, held the new mark and pole position.

The night before the race two-time winner Glenn (Fireball) Roberts received what he declared to be the most glowing tribute ever paid him in the 20 years he has been making racing history. Falstaff Brewing Corporation signed the four-time Darlington winner to a personal appearance contract that places him on the same team with Dizzy Dean, Pee Wee Reese, Red Grange, and John Lujack. Said

the Fireball, "This is a great break for stock car racing."

But, the next day the breaks were all missing, except for young Lorenzen. For 200 of the 300 miles he and Plymouth-driving Richard Petty traded the lead 10 times, before the Petty radiator started to leak and the engine overheated. That was the race.

Near the end, the Fireball was charging! Leader Lorenzen's tires were thin and the Old Pro sensed opportunity. From 24 seconds behind, the lavender "22" of Roberts closed the gap until but four seconds separated the pair. Then came the break. Two cars collided and out came the caution flag six laps from the finish.

The green flag came out on the next to last lap but the one break had done its work. Roberts took second money still four seconds behind.

Top left/Darlington Publicist Russ Catlin, Glenn "Fireball" Roberts, Schafer Distributing's Chris Yahnis, Darlington's President Bob Colvin.

Left/Falstaff's Bill Horne, "Fireball," Darlington's Bob Colvin.

Just takes time. Time and patience."

Ned Jarrett, another big name driver from the early 1960s, shared some quality time with Roberts that night as well. Jarrett earned fame again in the 1980s and '90s as a television racing analyst working for CBS and ESPN.

"The night before the accident, we sat out by the pool at the old Heart of Charlotte motel which was the key motel where most of the racing people stayed at, and we talked for a couple of hours," said Jarrett, who was a two-time series champion.

"It was a rewarding conversation as far as I was concerned because I never spent that much time with him. We talked fairly often about racing and about life, but he shared with me that night that he was planning to retire at the end of the year and he had the opportunity to become a spokesperson for Falstaff Beer. He was pretty excited about that. That was the first time I had heard of a NASCAR driver becoming a spokesperson for any product. I was excited for him. We talked about that quite a bit and his accomplishments and his approach to racing."

The lights went out early that night. Judy Judge was expecting the same old night-before-the-big-race routine. "Always, the night before a race, we slept in separate beds. Always," Judge said, explaining Roberts had a boxer's mentality. Boxers avoid sex before a prizefight fearing the excessive exercise will zap their energy level in the ring.

"We had a routine," she continued. "We'd get into bed, turn off the lights, then he would say – and I could count to 10 – he'd say, 'Honey, can you get me an aspirin?' So I would get up and get him an aspirin. I got him an aspirin that night and he patted his bed and said, 'Sleep here.'

"I said, 'But it's Saturday night.' He said, 'I don't care.' So I did. That was so strange. He told me he was going to make love to me like there was no tomorrow, and he did, and there wasn't."

1952
7 Starts, 0 Poles
1 Race Led
443 Laps, 15 Laps Led
0 Wins, Rank: 59
Winnings: $199

Lap 8

Charlotte Motor Speedway was never kind to Fireball Roberts, who had won at every other big asphalt track, including several times at mighty Daytona, on NASCAR's schedule.

In 1960 he crashed out of both NASCAR Grand National Series races, setting the tone of his relationship with the new track. He damn near lost his life there in 1961 during the National 400, Charlotte's second NASCAR race date in the fall.

Roberts' car lost power after his right front tire exploded off the rim and spun into the racing groove. His No. 22 Pontiac was t-boned on the passenger side by driver Bill Morgan, driving a Ford. It was a full-on, oh-shit, sheet-metal collision that looked so horrific the crowd of nearly 36,000 could only sit awash in silence. A feeling of dread swept over the grandstands as emergency crews tended to the two drivers.

"It was one of the most dramatic things I ever saw at the racetrack," Humpy Wheeler says today. "Fireball was leading the race and blew a right-front tire, which happened in those days when you ran hard. He crashed coming out the fourth turn.

"Morgan hit him right in the passenger door. It was as hard a lick as I have ever seen on a racetrack. The whole crowd quieted. The P.A. guy didn't say a word. There was just eerie silence. It was a terrible wreck. He wasn't moving. Everybody was fearing the worst at that point.

"Then Fireball shook it off and got out of the car and I've never seen an ovation like that, before or since. There was people who thought he had cheated death that day. His car owner [Smokey Yunick] took that car to a scrap iron place in town and had it crushed and took that metal cube back to Daytona. Smokey never wanted to look at that car again. If Fireball had taken that hit on the driver's side, then forget it, that would have been it."

Roberts didn't escape completely unscathed, later reporting that he picked slivers of shattered glass "from my neck and back for two weeks."

During his career, Roberts made nine starts at Charlotte and logged several respectable runs, including a couple of second-place finishes. Second place in racing? Dale Earnhardt used to grouse, "Second place means you were the first loser." That he had not conquered the big track, had not won at Charlotte, bothered Roberts like a sore tooth.

Roberts was going to make one last attempt to win at this track before hanging up his helmet and beginning his new life as a sports personality and taking Judy Judge as his wife. He wanted to go one more round and lock horns with his asphalt nemesis.

After his relaxing evening at the Heart of Charlotte, Roberts arrived at the track bright and early on race morning to avoid the throng of fans expected for the fifth annual World 600. One of his pet peeves was sitting in traffic. Roads around the Charlotte track would clog up with cars and nothing would move. They said there was one way in and no way out.

On the way to the track, Roberts detailed his strategy to Judge, who served as his sounding board for every topic under the sun.

Roberts always told Judge what he was going to do in the race so Judge wouldn't worry as she watched from the infield.

"He told me, 'I'm gonna hang back,' " Judge said. " 'It's a 600-mile race, I'll hang back, don't worry about it. The car will be good and the idiots will take each other out. I'll be lurking in back, and at 450 miles, I'll be on my way.' "

"He told me, 'It's 600 miles and I'm going to stay around 15th place. Don't worry.' He was not going to be anxious to be leading the race. He told me, 'I'm always careful. It's the other idiots who aren't careful.' So I knew he wasn't going to be dashing to the front. He always told me the first part of the race was always the most dangerous because the cars were packed so tight together."

After arriving at the track, they stayed in the car and talked some more. "He parked us in the infield and, as I always said, 'I'll see you in the winner's circle' and he walked away," she said. "He got about 30 feet away, turned around and came back, knelt down on one knee, kissed my hand and said, 'I really love you. You have made me very happy.' And I said, 'You are the love of my life.' He said, 'I know that and that means everything to me.'

"Somebody walked by and said, 'Fireball, you're gonna be late for the drivers' meeting.' He got up, walked away and came back to me again. I said, 'You are gonna be late.' He said, 'I want a blue bedroom. I want it to be blue.' And he said, 'I love you.' "

Somewhere between retiring to the room and making passionate, heart throbbing love, Roberts and Judge were looking at color patterns and furniture designs in a stack of home and design magazines. They were planning a major makeover for their house back in Daytona.

After finally leaving for the garage area, Roberts sought out his crew chief (chief mechanic for his car), Jack Sullivan, who Roberts fondly called "Sully." Roberts had hopped to this new team about a third of the way into the 1963 season; leaving car owner/crew chief Banjo Matthews to take a factory ride with Holman-Moody Racing, which was thick in Ford dollars.

Roberts' race car was easy to spot on the track. Not only did it carry his signature No. 22 competition number, but it had an attention-getting lavender hue. Roberts talked at length with Sullivan about the smallest details of his car that morning because he wanted to be fully prepared for the task at hand – go the distance in NASCAR's punishing marathon and be in a position to win this damn race and erase that one pesky zero off his win column.

Some say Roberts planned to retire as a driver immediately after the World 600 while others maintain he wanted to participate in the Fourth of July Firecracker 400 at Daytona and the Southern 500 in Darlington, South Carolina, on Labor Day that year before calling it

quits. Either way, 1964 would be his last year as a race car driver. He was looking at a whole new lifestyle in 1965 – new wife, new house, new outlook on life.

He had qualified 11th in the 44-car field, which means in individual speed runs over the 1.5-mile course, he produced the 11th-fastest speed on the track. Jim Paschal, who went on to win that day in a Plymouth, was to his immediate right on the grid. Junior Johnson and David Pearson, a pair of "good ol' boys" from the Carolinas, were on the row ahead of Roberts, driving a Ford and Dodge, respectively. Another row up, was "Gentleman" Ned Jarrett, the 1961 Grand National champion in a glistening '64 Ford.

Before the race, Roberts approached Pearson, who had won the 1961 World 600 as a rookie. Roberts ran second that day, the "first loser" by two laps. "I remember the last words he ever spoke to me," Pearson said years later. "He said, 'Now Dub, a lot of these other guys will to go to the front right away. Take it easy. Just lay back. And just be careful.' "

That was Roberts' race strategy because his sixth sense, his racing sense, had sniffed a puff of danger in the air. Before he strapped into his car, Roberts was going to play it safe and do exactly what he told Pearson to do during their short, pit road conversation – ride easy and lay back. Races are not won in the opening laps.

Decades later, at the same track, another driver just released from the infield care center after crashing explained the pitfalls of racing in the wrong pack of cars at Charlotte. "If you race with squirrels," he said, "expect to get your nuts cracked."

Roberts was easy to spot from the grandstands during pre-race ceremonies. First, he was taller than most drivers, a relative giant at 6-foot-2. And, he wore a custom-made, stylish driving suit, one of the few drivers back then who had competition fashion sense. There was only one problem with the uniform – it was not fireproof. Drivers would dip the T-shirts, pants, coveralls or overalls they planned to wear during the race in a drum of fire retardant chemical (boric acid), then hang them on the nearest chain-link fence to dry.

"It was as much of a fire retardant as we had at that time," said Bill Gazaway, who started out as a racer only to become a NASCAR official later in life.

Roberts dismissed the pre-race ritual because the awful smell of the dried solution would trigger an asthma attack. At the time, there was no alternative solution. Roberts struggled with the chronic

respiratory ailment all his life, even though he chain-smoked cigarettes and had a regular workout regime which included lifting weights to build stamina.

Race cars of the day did not have the creature comfort of power steering like today's machines. Drivers say hustling one of those gigantic brutes around an asphalt track was like arm wrestling a bear for four hours. It's no wonder Roberts, and other drivers of the time, had Popeye-like forearms.

It was time to race. Forty-four stock cars in field for the 400-lap endurance test over the 1.5-mile course. There was a real stir in the air as the drivers ignited their thundering V8 engines, which caused the ground to quake and goose bumps to rise on the arms of young and old alike.

Judge watched the proceedings nervously from a perch in the garage area. She would only have to go through this nerve-rattling ritual maybe once, or twice, more.

"I hated it, absolutely hated it," she said. "I was not very nice to be around. I was always worried about him."

Judge's dread grew far worse after Joe Weatherly died in a wreck at Riverside, Calif., earlier in 1964. Roberts and Weatherly were good friends. "When Joe got killed, that was terrible," she said. "I knew it could happen to Glenn. He always tried to make me feel more at ease before he would leave me before a race."

And, they were off!

The green flag waved from the starter's stand at the start-finish line. The rumbling wave of cars gained speed in Turn 1 and by Turn 3, they were at full song, a parade of the most modern, and deadly, racing machines turning laps in excess of 140 mph.

It didn't take long for problems to start. Several of these gas-snorting fire breathers made a hasty retreat from the track with an assortment of mechanical problems. The stress of high-speed laps took its toll on eight machines in only the first five laps of competition. Stock car racing in those days not only turned nerves brittle, but was hell on cars not maximized for this tour of duty.

Young Buddy Baker was the ninth car out when he slapped at the wheel and yanked his Dodge off the track after laying down just six laps, his motor hot enough to boil a kettle of water.

Lap 8.

"I saw this terrible smoke," said Judge, who turned to a friend, her face completely pale. " 'It's Glenn. I know it is Glenn.' "

Judy Judge, just weeks away from being married, literally watched her future rise up in smoke.

1953

2 Starts, 0 Poles
1 Race Led
352 Laps, 41 Laps Led
0 Wins, Rank: 132
Winnings: $365

1800°

Some have described the accident as the worst, nightmarish and ghastly they could ever imagine happening to a race car driver. Everything that could go wrong went terribly wrong on Lap 8 of the 1964 World 600.

It started out as one of those typical "racing deals" when two cars make contact, then go spinning like tops down the asphalt track. That is exactly what happened to Ned Jarrett and Junior Johnson, two of NASCAR's marquee names.

As the field of cars rocketed through Turns 1 and 2, the Fords driven by Jarrett and Johnson were racing side-by-side, just a few seconds away from becoming one of stock car racing's most sickening afternoons of competition. It also produced the most valiant, unselfish and courageous act in racing history.

According to various reports of the day, and modern day interviews with Jarrett and Johnson, their cars were running so close that they hooked bumpers and became entwined as they rumbled through the banking.

Johnson was attempting to pass Jarrett for position on the outside racing lane. Johnson said his car ran over a bump on the course which caused him to make initial contact with Jarrett. "Me and Ned got tangled up coming off of that second turn," Johnson says today.

"It was just a racing accident," said Jarrett, who has replayed the accident over and over again in his mind for the last 40 years. "Junior Johnson and I came together. He was trying to pass me and our cars touched." Later that year, Fred Lorenzen, Roberts' teammate, said a "gust of wind" twisted Johnson's car out of control "before he could do anything about it."

When they reached the end of the turn, the Siamese stock cars separated in a cloud of tire smoke. Both began to spin uncontrollably down the 1,360-foot backstretch, Johnson to the outside and Jarrett toward the infield. Jarrett's Ford smashed into a concrete wall designed to keep race cars from rampaging through the infield where many spectators watch the races. The contact was extremely hard; his metal gas tank busted open and the uncontained fuel immediately caught fire.

"It happened very quickly," Jarrett said. "You don't have time to get scared. You are wrapped up in what you are doing. The first thing that comes to your mind is, 'This thing going to stay on its wheels?' The next thing is, 'Where am I going to get hit? Am I going to hit the wall? Is somebody going to t-bone me in the door?' That's the biggest thing you didn't want to happen, to have somebody t-bone you in the door.

"Once I slid down to the inside, I didn't have that concern. I knew the thing was on fire pretty quickly because it burst the fuel tank on my car. I could see it was on fire in my rear-view mirror. So my biggest concern in that wreck was, 'Get this thing stopped and get out of here.' I didn't know what was going on as far as Junior or Fireball was concerned."

Driver Darel Dieringer and Fireball Roberts were driving the cars immediately behind Johnson and Jarrett, and rapidly closing on the mayhem happening only a few hundred feet in front of them.

"I saw Johnson's car back out of the (tire) smoke and head toward the outside wall, so I closed my eyes and went under him," Dieringer told the *Charlotte News* in the days following the accident. "I couldn't see for the smoke from Jarrett's car." As Dieringer approached the accident site at nearly full speed, he was overtaken by Roberts' Ford. "He passed me," Dieringer said, "backing up." Roberts was going as fast as Dieringer, only out of control in reverse.

The combination of tire smoke and smolder from Jarrett's burning car made it nearly impossible to see, so to avoid t-boning his friends, Roberts apparently turned hard left on his steering wheel to intentionally spin his car.

According to Roberts' father, Edward Glenn Sr., his son was hoping to loop his Ford to avoid contact with the other cars in the area and come to rest out of harm's way. The *Charlotte News* reported that Roberts' car traveled sideways and diagonally some 300 feet before the initial impact.

Roberts' car spun off the backstretch and into the abutment of the infield concrete wall, the same wall Jarrett had struck at speed. Roberts hit with such horrific force that his car caromed off the wall and twisted upside down, bouncing 28 feet beyond the point of impact. Since the gas tank was positioned in the trunk section of the car, it had busted wide open and exploded. His tank was ruptured and burning gas was gushing into the driver's compartment where Roberts was strapped in the seat, upside down.

"That opening in the wall was, I'm thinking, like two-thirds of the way down the backstretch," Jarrett said. "A lot of tracks had those openings back then. It was where traffic could go across to the infield. They didn't have a gate or anything to close off the inside wall. They had a gate for the outside wall. They didn't have anything for the inside walls to protect that opening."

39

Roberts' car came to rest 30 feet behind Jarrett's burning Ford. Now both cars were ablaze and a column of dark, ominous smoke formed over the scene of the crash. The fire had plenty to feed from. Those cars each carried 22 gallons of gas and it was so early in the race most of it was still in the tanks.

"We didn't have fuel cells so when it did hit that abutment in the wall, it not only burst the gas tank but it broke the firewall," Jarrett said. "So when he flipped upside down, there was gasoline running down inside the car. It was a situation where everything seemed to go wrong."

Greg Fielden, a noted stock car racing historian, was 13 years old and sitting next to his father in prime grandstand seats that afternoon. "I saw a big, black mushroom cloud," Fielden said. "We didn't have radio scanners in those days and didn't know who it was at first. My dad was trying to determine who was missing when they came past where we were sitting. I realized Junior was missing and my dad said, 'Fireball isn't out there either.' "

"From where I was, I couldn't see the wreck," Judy Judge said. "I was on top of the Firestone truck and there was a mound of dirt in the infield and I couldn't see past it, but I knew it was him because I didn't see his car come around the track."

Max Muhleman, one of Roberts' best friends and the auto racing writer for the *Charlotte News*, was sitting high atop the grandstands in a radio booth offering commentary to a local radio station.

"There was a spin," he told the *Charlotte Observer*, 34 years later. "You could see them but you couldn't see them real clearly. Then there was this huge plume of smoke, a tremendous gas fire. I got this sick feeling in my throat."

Noted racing journalist Bob Meyers, who was Muhleman's sidekick at the *News* in those days, watched the menacing scene unfold from above the grandstands. "I was in an old wooden press box there at the speedway," he said. "It was an open-air deal, but it was high enough that you could see all the way over there…I saw it from start to finish, but I couldn't exactly tell what happened. It happened so fast. Nobody was really expecting something like that."

At the accident site, Jarrett had unbuckled his safety harness and slithered out of his burning auto. Disoriented, he stumbled away from the crash scene and propped himself up against the concrete wall. "I sat down on the wall," Jarrett said. "Immediately, I saw Fireball trying to get out of his car and ran over there."

Roberts had come free of his seat belts and was attempting to crawl out of the inferno surrounding him. Apparently, one his legs or one of his feet was pinned or hooked to something inside the car, because he struggled to get out. For Jarrett, it was like a glimpse of hell, as Roberts looked up, raised an arm and pleaded, "Oh my God, Ned, help me, I'm on fire."

"I grabbed him by the arms under his shoulders and jerked him out of the car," Jarrett said. "Then we started to tear his uniform off. It wasn't long before the safety people got there. They got there fairly quick. In one sense, it seemed like an eternity, but it wasn't long. It was only a minute or so, but a lot of damage could be done in that period of time."

Gasoline vapor can ignite at about 280 degrees. Once a gas fire starts, it can reach temperatures of 1,800 degrees. Roberts was soaked in gasoline from his back to his ankles and his driving suit offered no protection.

After Jarrett had risked his own life to pull Roberts from the sheet metal carnage, fireman Gene Deese, who was assigned to that area of the race course, helped Jarrett start ripping the clothes off the driver's body. Roberts' tailor-made suit proved to be a hindrance during the rescue.

"One of the problems in the accident was that he was such a classy guy and he wore that tailor made uniform, which was very hard to take off when you need to in a hurry," Jarrett said. "It had zippers on the

Facts Behind Roberts Wreck

GLENN (FIREBALL) ROBERTS, critically burned in the May 24th World 600 late model auto race at the Charlotte Motor Speedway, continues to make slow, but sure progress toward recovery . . . The battle will not be an easy or a rapid one . . . At this stage, his physicians will not say how long they think Roberts will be hospitalized . . . Meanwhile, the veteran NASCAR driver could perhaps write a book on some of the things that have happened to him since the accident . . . For one thing, Roberts' fan mail has been tremendously heavy . . . More than 5,000 letters and cards have been received during the first two weeks of his hospitalization . . . The mail has come from all over the world, including Germany, Mexico and Canada . . . One Mexican race fan even suggested that Roberts take up bull fighting because "it's safer." . . . Any number of rabbit's feet and good luck charms have come from well wishers to Roberts' Memorial Hospital room, where visitors are restricted to members of his family, and only then when Roberts' ask for them.

* * *

THERE ARE SEVERAL facts about the Roberts accident which have not previously been related . . . According to Fireball's father, Glen Roberts Sr., Roberts spun his car intentionally after the cars of Ned Jarrett and Junior Johnson collided at the head of the backstretch and went spinning wildly down the long, fast shute. As Mr. Roberts related, Fireball was trailing Darel Dieringer, who was a couple hundred feet behind Johnson and Jarrett . . . Seeing the spinning cars ahead, being partially blinded by Dieringer's car and not knowing whether he or Dieringer could get past without crashing, Roberts decided to spin his mount, hoping he could wind up on the apron of the track and continue in the race . . . Dieringer, meanwhile, has said, "I saw Johnson's car back out of the smoke and head toward the outside wall, so I closed my eyes and went under him. I couldn't see for the smoke from Jarrett's car. All I could do was hope, and I was lucky." . . . Jarrett's car had burst into flames, and gas from his tank had set the inside of the track on fire . . . Roberts' car, which Dieringer said "passed me backing up," hit the end of a retaining wall going backwards, flipped upside down and landed 28 feet from where it hit the wall . . . Jarrett, whose car had stopped about 30 feet beyond where Roberts' car landed, jumped out of his burning machine and assisted Roberts . . . Also quickly to the scene were seven track firemen, who were stationed about 30 feet from where Roberts' car landed . . . One fireman, Gene Deese, helped Jarrett remove Roberts' racing uniform, which was turned over to Earl Kelley, speedway promotions director.

sleeves and zippers on the legs and zippers up the sides."

"I think if he had on looser type clothes, it would have been easier to get them off, flame proof or not," Jarrett added. "The sleeves were banded like some jackets are, with an elastic type band; the legs as well. Everywhere there was an opening, at the sleeves, neck, bottom of his pants, that's where it was burning. It was hard to get that thing off in a hurry. We both got burned trying to get it off as quickly as we could."

Johnson, who had spun farther up the track, was not injured and climbed from his crippled machine. He started to walk back to check on Jarrett and Roberts. Then he started to run. He was horrified at the scene unfolding before him.

"I was walking back there when it busted into flames," Johnson said. "They started to put the fire out and Fireball got out of the car. Ned was there to help him get away from the fire, where they could get the fire put out on his uniform and stuff. It was basically a chaotic thing.

"Nobody could really get to Fireball early enough to keep him from getting burnt. When he undone his seat belt, the fuel had run out of the tank into the top of the car and it was sort of like pooling in there. When he come out, he was a solid blaze of fire. He was saturated with fuel when he come out of that car. He was allergic to that stuff we'd fireproof our uniforms in at that time but in his case I don't think it would have mattered. It was terrible."

Johnson is probably right. Driver Dale Earnhardt Jr. experienced a cockpit gas fire while competing in a non-NASCAR event in 2004. He was wearing a modern, fire-proof suit but still suffered patches of burns to various parts of his body. "The wreck was fiery and hot," Earnhardt Jr. said of his accident. "The pain was intense. I remember everything about the wreck…It was quite an experience and not one I want to go through again."

Jarrett's courage to pull Roberts from the flaming sheet metal carnage was extraordinary. "You don't think about it," said Jarrett, who suffered severe burns to his hands and forehead while trying to rescue Roberts. "There was fire all around his car. You don't think about that. You just go in there and do what you have to do try to help a fellow man. It's a human being and you want to help. That's what it is. In that particular case, it was a friend."

Two-way radios were not widely used in those days but the competitors still in the race knew exactly what had happened – either Jarrett or Roberts had been burned bad, really bad.

Curtis Crider, who finished 11th that day, had a look at the crash site as the cars continued to circulate the track under caution and felt sick to his stomach.

"I had to pit and get a relief driver," Crider said. "I had to let Doug Cox drive until the next pit stop, until I could settle down. I felt sick. I was thinking to myself, 'What the hell are we doing out here?' I didn't know it was Fireball at first. I knew it was one of two. With the fire and all you couldn't tell. There was 44 gallons of fuel burning right close together. To see someone hurt like that…"

Crider could not finish the sentence.

Said former NASCAR official Bill Gazaway, who was manning pit road that day: "It wasn't the best place to be or the most pleasant."

After realizing Roberts was involved in the accident, Judge hurried to the infield care center where she found Jarrett. "Ned's uniform was off, he was in his white undershirt," Judge remembers. "Ned told me, 'He's alive. I got him out of the car. He's alive. He's over in the infield hospital.' "

"It was like I was trying to run under water," she said. "I could not go fast enough. Gene White, who represented Firestone at the tracks, met me at the door to the hospital. I asked him, 'Where is he?' Gene told me, 'They are taking him by helicopter to the hospital.' I didn't faint, but I couldn't stand up. My legs would not carry me. Gene picked me up and put me on a stretcher and a doctor came over and put something under my nose. He told me they had taken Glenn by helicopter to the hospital. I was hysterical. I looked at Gene and asked him if he was taking me over or would I have to drive. Gene was a former race driver and owned a Firestone store. Glenn and Gene were dear friends."

There are no words to describe the emotions that coursed through Judge's mind and body at that moment in time. All she wanted to do was see, and touch, and talk to her fiancé. Roberts was transported to Charlotte Memorial Hospital's emergency room for preliminary treatment. Judge raced to the hospital to be with the love of her life but was restrained in a waiting area.

"Gene put me in his car and drove me to the hospital. It seemed like forever to get there. They brought me a bag with his shoes and his watch and his ring. I had his wallet and all that stuff. All I kept thinking was, 'He's going to have an asthma attack.' And I wanted to let them know he had asthma and I was trying to tell everybody who would listen he had asthma. Finally, somebody said, 'Give us his inhaler.' "

After several hours, one of Roberts' attending physicians found Judge and delivered the dire news. Roberts had severe burns to 75 percent of his body. Most of the skin on his legs and back had been completely burned off his body.

"They put Gene and me in a room and we sat there for a long time. Finally, a doctor came and told me he was severely burned and they didn't know if he was going to live and I needed to call whoever needed to be called. I told the doctor, 'You've got to let me see him. He's got to know I'm here. I've got to see his face. He's got to see my face.' And they wouldn't. They said they would let me know. I called his mother and daddy and told them it was very bad. By that time Glenn's uncle Herbert, who was flying planes for Gene, had come to the hospital. I gave him the keys to the airplane and told him to get Glenn's mother and father in Daytona. That's the last time I saw the keys to the plane.

"People were coming from the racetrack. Oh God, I don't know who all was there. Everybody. Gene White did all the talking to the people coming from the track. He kept me in that room by myself. I could not talk. About 4 o'clock that afternoon, the doctor came in to get me. He said they were going to take him up to the intensive care unit and I could go with him if I could control myself. He said they did not think he was going to live. I said, 'Where is he?' They had him on a gurney right outside that room I was in. Everybody backed away when I came out of the room. He had a towel up to his shoulders. His face looked sunburned, real sunburned. The tops of his shoulders didn't look burned at all. I leaned over and said, 'I'm here.' He said, 'I took a terrible whack.'

"A nurse came up and said, 'Mr. Roberts, I'm going to give you a tetanus shot and it's going to hurt like hell.' He told her, 'I'm gonna be sore all over tomorrow anyway so go ahead.' He gave him the shot in the shoulder and he never flinched. A doctor was leaned over on one side of his head and I was on the other, and they started pushing him to an elevator. Glenn told me then, 'Whatever you do, don't let me go to sleep. I'm afraid I'll go into shock and won't wake up. Don't let me go to sleep.' I said, 'I promise you, I will not let you sleep.' He said, 'I don't want you out of my sight.' And I said, 'I'll be right there with you.' They took him up to this room and they wouldn't let me go in when they put him on the bed. When they let me in, he was on his tummy. I sat on the floor, under his face, so he could see me. We talked all night. They would come in and fuss with him and do things to him but I couldn't see it because I was on the floor. He would start to nod off and I'd call his name and he would wake up.

"Three or four times, they told me I had to leave when they turned him and that's when I'd go to the waiting room and there were 50 or more people in there. I may have talked to them, but I don't remember. The doctor came back out and said he wanted to talk to me and kept calling me 'Mrs. Roberts.' I said, 'I'm not. I'm his fiancée.' He said, 'I don't care who you are, you are the one he wants.' The doctor then told me, 'We think he's blind. He's probably blind.' I told them he wasn't blind. I was looking at his face all night and he was not blind."

Edward Glenn Sr. said he heard about the accident during a radio bulletin at his Daytona Beach home and placed phone calls to Memorial Hospital and Charlotte Motor Speedway. The news was not good.

"They told me he was critical, that he could die at any time," Roberts Sr. said many years later. Roberts' parents flew to Charlotte later that night and arrived at the hospital around midnight.

Pamela Roberts, Fireball's only child, remembers listening to the racing folk who assembled at the hospital in the days following the accident. She told the *Charlotte Observer* she remembers overhearing Buddy Baker say, "If that had been anybody but Fireball Roberts, he'd be dead."

The hospital was besieged by upset race fans. Normally, two operators manned the hospital switchboard. Three additional operators had to be added to handle the crush of daily phone calls. Cards and letters poured in from around the world, including one from Mexico. The writer suggested Roberts take up bull fighting, the *Charlotte News* reported, because "it's safer." Bob Meyers said he vividly recalls the chaos at the hospital: "All those cards people sent, a whole bed full of cards that his fiancée Judy Judge was keeping at the time and the hospital reports; they had to ask people not to call the hospital and they started issuing bulletins on him, sometimes three times a day, reporting his condition."

Four days later the hospital released a detailed description of Roberts' injuries, which was excerpted and reprinted by the *Observer* 25 years later:

> He has burns over about 75% of his body, 35% of them are third-degree burns…A rule of thumb is that it is usually fatal if a person has third-degree burns over 50%…The deepest burns are on the legs and arms… Roberts' body and its normal function suffered a severe shock. Our job had been to restore those functions and keep them going…He's in a Stryker frame; a type of bed which allows us to turn him over without moving him bodily, when we have to change his dressings.
>
> He has been conscious throughout. His spirits are reasonable…He has talked of racing one time… We feel that we will be able to graft skin from his abdomen, where he escaped burns…We're happy with

his progress, but the man is very, very sick…

Barring a tragic infection, this man will come through…"

The tug-of-war for Roberts' life had begun. Doctors, medicine and Roberts' sheer will on one end the rope; the cold fingers of fate pulling relentlessly from the other side. All Judy Judge could do was sit in the middle of this titanic struggle and pray. And cry.

1954
5 Starts, 0 Poles
0 Races Led
811 Laps, 0 Laps Led
0 Wins, Rank: 22
Winnings: $1,080

A Piece of the Action

How does a man, who was born in rural Tavares, Florida, end up with an unusual and catchy nickname and become a nationally known sports figure?

It was an interesting journey.

Edward Glenn Roberts, Jr. was born in his grandmother's house on Jan. 20, 1929. He was the first of three children for Edward Glenn and Doris Roberts, who was just 18 when she brought Glenn Jr. into the world. Two years later the Robertses had their second child, daughter JoAnne.

"We didn't live there very long," said JoAnne Roberts. "We moved to Apopka in 1933."

That's where Roberts Sr. began working for a company that manufactured wooden crates to transport citrus fruit. Over the years he became a superintendent at this sawmill and built a brick house for his young family on the north side of Apopka.

Around the house, young Roberts was known as Glenn Jr. As

brother and sister started grade school, JoAnne affectionately called her older brother "Bubby," a nickname she uses even to this day.

Glenn Jr. could be described as an adventurous child limited in physical activities by chronic asthma attacks. He stayed inside the house more than other kids his age because of his condition. He wasn't a shut-in, but his movements were restricted by his loving, fearful mother.

"In his youth, he was a little ol' skinny nothing," JoAnne says with a laugh, then reflecting on a more serious note, "Bubby was a loner. He didn't have many friends. He liked his privacy."

To replace afternoon romps with other neighborhood children, Glenn Jr. spent more time reading than most kids his age and started a stamp collection. He very much enjoyed piecing together model cars and planes. He was especially intrigued with airplanes.

"Even though you needed that stinky glue, which wasn't good for his asthma, to build model airplanes, he would build them and enter them at the county fair and won blue ribbons," JoAnne says. "He read constantly, because what else could he do? He was a good student."

As Glenn Jr. got older, he also became bolder. His father remembers taking the wife to the movies in Orlando and coming home to find his 10-year-old son had made an unauthorized romp on the family farming equipment.

"We'd come home to find that he'd been driving my tractor out through the woods," Glenn Sr. said.

JoAnne says when Bubby was around 12, he was out in the yard hacking weeds with a machete and split open the middle finger on his left hand. He saw what looked like white string coming out of the gaping wound and took it upon himself to cut it off. It was the tendon in his finger. From that day on that finger was always slightly bent downward.

Years later "machete" became a couple's code word for Glenn Jr. and Judy. "I used to say 'machete' in any conversation he was having with anyone, and it was the code word that he was saying something dumb or wrong," she says today.

Roberts carried another physical reminder of his childhood into adulthood. JoAnne and he went to a public spring on a hot summer day in their early teens, before Glenn Jr. could drive. He was goofing around, slipped, fell and split both his front teeth.

"It was a natural spring and it's where we all went to swim," JoAnne said. "It also had a man-made pool and they put this big, metal elephant out there for kids to play on. Bubby tried to stand up on it, fell, and hit his front teeth. He broke one tooth in half and another at an angle, that's why he had that little gold thing on his left tooth. I had to call Daddy to come get us. It was very painful because the nerve was hanging out of that one tooth."

It was about this time that Glenn Jr. picked up the nickname that would stick to him like day-old pancake syrup on a paper plate. It was the name he carried for the rest of his life, which would become the tragic irony of his death.

JoAnne says her brother never participated in organized sports except playing running back (she thinks) for the Apopka High School Blue Darters football team as a sophomore, which proved to be an exercise in frustration.

"He'd go out and play, then come back and get some oxygen and go back out," she said. "Other than that, he never played any sports in a uniform."

"He wanted to play football like any other kid, but it was too strenuous for him," Glenn Sr. said years later. "He had the size and ability. If he hadn't been handicapped by the asthma, he might have wound up as a professional football player."

There have been long debates on the origin of Glenn Jr.'s nickname. Max Muhleman sets the record straight. He befriended the young driver in 1958. Roberts had just moved up to NASCAR's Grand National Series ranks the year before. Muhleman says Roberts received the celebrated nickname during a sandlot baseball game. Roberts was 15 years old and tossing some heat from the mound that spring day.

"Some kids were playing baseball on a sandlot diamond and they needed a pitcher," Muhleman said. "A big Greek boy was catching when Glenn sent a high, hard one sailing toward the plate. 'Hey!' whistled the catcher, 'you're a real *fireball*.' "

From that day forward, Edward Glenn Roberts Jr. was known to all as Fireball, a name he nurtured as a youth and used effectively during his race car driving career. It was a name he secretly disdained as he grew older. To competitors in the garage area, he was simply "Balls" because of his courage behind the wheel of a stock car machine. He didn't like that name much either.

When Glenn Jr. was old enough to drive, he wasn't satisfied with the family sedan. He put together his own highway hybrid, a '37 Chevrolet coupe powered by a big-ass, Cadillac engine. At night and on weekends, he would drag race with friends on U.S. Highway 441, a little-used asphalt artery that connected the tiny villages of Apopka and Mount Dora.

His friend, Curt Haygood, told a Florida newspaper that "You probably could have heard us coming 10 miles away" and "We'd fly down that road."

In 1945 Glenn Sr. made a decision that probably led to his son becoming a race car driver. Tired of the sawmill, he bought a small apartment building, called the Cactus Courts, a block off the beach in Daytona Beach when his son was 16 years old. By that time, the Roberts family had another son, Tommy, who was a toddler.

Glenn Jr. was not happy about the move to the east Florida coast. JoAnne says that she and Bubby would ride over to Apopka "almost every weekend" after moving to the shoreline. "In Apopka, we were big fish in a little pond and in Daytona, we were little fish in a big pond."

Fireball enrolled at Seabreeze High School, which was several blocks from his new home, but never finished the 11th grade. Disenchanted by the move, he dropped out of school and enlisted in the Air Force at the age of 17; he was assigned to a base in Texas.

"He was in the Air Force for 90 days then they gave up on him," JoAnne says. "They gave him a medical discharge because of his asthma. He was in the hospital most of the time he was out there in Texas."

When he returned to Daytona Beach, he enrolled at a local vocational school and earned a G.E.D. and attended graduation ceremonies with his old classmates at Apopka High in 1947.

The next two years, Roberts attended the University of Florida in Gainesville where he first began pursuing a degree in aeronautical engineering, later switching to mechanical engineering. He would come home often on weekends – make that *race* home. Some of his banzai runs between Gainesville and Daytona Beach are the stuff of legends, like *Dukes of Hazzard* crazy.

His favorite route home was Highway 100 which ran east-west from Gainesville to Bunnell (north of Daytona) where he would catch U.S. 1 south into Daytona Beach. His sister described the car as a "souped-up, '39 Ford."

"About every time he came through Bunnell, the police would stop him," JoAnne said. "I drove that car a few times. You had to drive it fast or it would conk out on you. The sound of that car embarrassed me to death, it was so loud."

Fireball's college roommate, George McClure, told the *Orlando Sentinel* that "he had this hot rod and man, it would move."

"If you were smart, you'd be hanging on tight the whole ride. If you were a religious man, you'd be praying," McClure said, adding that even a police roadblock could not stop this man of speed.

"I figured he was caught, but Fireball just kind of slips off the road and on the shoulder and sort of up on the edge of the ditch and right on around them," McClure described. "And we're going 105 mph. I told him, 'The hell with this, I'm not riding with you anymore.' "

Edward Glenn Roberts Jr. was not cut out for the college life. He had too much energy to sit in a chair and do a whole lot of thinking. In life, Fireball majored in racing and minored in women, and there was precious little room for books, formal learning and such.

"I think he had a 'D' average in college," JoAnne said. "But he was far from dumb."

The man responsible for Fireball's poor study habits was most likely Marshall Teague, who owned a service station near the Roberts' house. Teague mentored many a young man with oil running through their veins. Teague had several work bays and allowed young speed demons to tweak their cars in his garage.

Teague, who was about 10 years older than Roberts, scored seven NASCAR Grand National Series victories and made two starts in the prestigious Indianapolis 500. This guy was all about racing and offered Roberts inspiration and motivation to pursue a race car driving career.

"Marshall and Glenn were

good friends," said Bob Laney, who helped work on Roberts' cars in the late 1940s. "In the back of the service station, Marshall probably had eight stalls with all kinds of stuff in there. I pumped gas there for a while. It was a real half-assed job.

"I'd help him on the race cars and I'd tow the car for him to out-of-town races," Laney continued. "I had a '40 Ford coupe and we used that to tow Glenn's race cars with. That eventually turned into a race car. I'd help him as a friend. I got married in '50 and couldn't go off with him too much."

In 1964 Roberts told *Sports Illustrated* that when he first caught the racing bug, Teague "helped me a lot, and so did other mechanics around town."

Young Roberts had done some amateur dirt-track oval racing with his hot rod at horse tracks and fairground facilities in Central and North Florida and was ready to tackle a bigger challenge – competing in the 1947 modified race on the Daytona Beach & Road Course.

The old Daytona course was spectacular. Two miles of A1A blacktop going south, a cut in the sand dunes, followed by a two-mile jaunt north up the beach, where drivers would make a hard left back through the dunes to return to the asphalt portion of the course. The power slides through the North Turn were things of beauty.

Because of the unique venue, it was a very popular event, attracting a mob of spectators each winter. Fireball wanted a piece of this action bad but his father would not sign the permission slip required by drivers under the age of 21. He had to get his mother, Doris, to sign the paperwork.

Also signed up for the '47 race was a young guy named Irwin Spiers from Jacksonville, fresh out of service to the U.S. Navy. He fancied a life as a race car driver and his friends called him "Speedy."

"I thought I wanted to be a race car driver," Spiers said. "I had high hopes of being one and I entered a car in the Daytona race. It didn't take much of anything to enter, just go down there and tell them you wanted to race."

It was that tricky South Turn, the one the drivers used to get back to the beach-side half of the course, which gave Spiers more than a little trouble that afternoon.

"I went into that turn a little deeper each time until I thought I was getting it about as good as anybody," Spiers said. "One time I went in there a little too hard and the front end of that old car took a big push and sailed right off the track."

Spiers' flight was much like that of the Wright brothers at Kitty Hawk, North Carolina – short but dramatic. His car launched off the track, sailed high into the air then landed into a flat, sandy area near some grandstands. His only injury was bruised pride.

"I ended up in the palmettos near a grandstand they had out there," he said. "The car landed on its feet and I sat there a minute and got my senses together and climbed out. I couldn't go anywhere, so I sat up on the roof of my car with my feet on the trunk lid to watch the rest of the race.

"About 10 laps later, another car comes sailing off the turn and lands right beside me, like six feet away from my car. Out crawls Fireball Roberts. He got up on my car and we sat there and talked during the rest of the race."

The two men crossed paths quite a bit at regional short tracks over the next few years but their relationship was solidified one spring day in 1950.

Roberts was 21 and attending the University of Florida. By chance, he ended up in the same class as Spiers. One thing led to another and before you could say "Oh shit!" Fireball and Speedy were heading for the exit during a particularly boring classroom session.

"It was springtime," Spiers said. "The birds were singing, the windows were open, the breeze was blowing, you know, the sun was shining. We looked at each other and said, 'What the heck are we doing here? We need to be doing something more interesting than this.' So we got up and walked out of class."

The female professor – Spiers figures she was in her early 30s – asked where they were going. "Fireball turned around and said, 'Up yours grandma. We're going racing,' " Spiers says with a hearty laugh more than 50 years later. "Can you imagine calling a woman in her 30s grandma? But to us, she was a much older lady."

Damn academia and conventional wisdom. When he left that classroom, Edward Glenn Roberts Jr., a.k.a. Fireball, had became a race car driver.

1955
2 Starts, 1 Pole
1 Race Led
69 Laps, 4 Laps Led
0 Wins, Rank: 201
Winnings: $140

'It's Like A Drea Come True'—Roberts

By ROB DESIDERIO

"Boy, when I got by that one, whew!" chortled Glenn (Fireball) Roberts with a mock shiver as he recalled his mental state on the 188th lap of his record smashing ride to victory yesterday in the Daytona 500.

Even in the first jubilance of winning the big one, Roberts couldn't forget his heartbreaking loss of last year's race when his crankshaft broke with only 13 laps to go.

"I just didn't know if I would make it," cried Fireball. "I really sweated out those last 10 laps. It's like a dream come true. I'm just so happy I can't really believe it's happened."

Roberts' first thought was for Robert (Junior) Johnson, 1960 winner of the 500, who played frontrunners' draft tag with Fireball until the 83rd lap, when his car was stopped by

1962 Plymouth into contention and second place after a fast pit stop in the 130th lap, Roberts was surprised to learn that anybody thought Petty had a chance.

"He didn't put any pressure on me," flatly maintained Roberts. "If he had ever got out from behind me . . ." added Roberts, alluding to his eight mile an hour edge in top speed over Petty. "In fact, I slowed down the last 50 miles. The only time I went flat

★

Fireball's Wife In Joyous Tears

Crying with joy, Doris Roberts said after her husband's 500 victory

out was with Junior on I breathed the turns.

"But I'll say this, if ard Petty did a won driving. He just drov that car. He must ha about five miles an h

Richard's only con livered with a wry "I was waiting for h up."

Fireball did have moments. "I ran out e on the backstretch figured the car would on a tankful of gas. It we got only 98 and I h in to the pits on the stops." Roberts pitted and 80th laps.

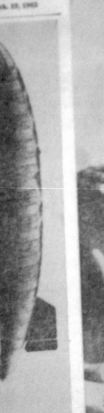

ONA BEACH
MORNING JOURNAL
Mon., Feb. 19, 1962

LAP AND HE'S WON IT!

Be Careful What You Wish For

Doris McConnell loved to talk about the time she met a dashing, young race car driver from Florida at a dirt track near her home in Kannapolis, North Carolina.

She told the story to family, friends, acquaintances, people at parties and reporters, looking for feature fodder for the newspaper society page.

One such story ran in *The Daily Independent*, the newspaper that services Kannapolis, a short drive north of Charlotte. If this small town has a familiar ring, it was home to racing great Dale Earnhardt and several other racing types.

Fifty years ago, Kannapolis was a depressed textile industrial center, offering low paying jobs to men and women of limited education. For instance, Earnhardt's father, Ralph, worked in a mill as a "lint head" until he accumulated enough racing equipment to make it a full-time venture.

Doris McConnell grew up in this area, graduating from J.W.

Cannon High school in 1946, then took a job as a tabulator in a Cannon Mills office.

In this low-income region, where a section of town has automotive-related street names, race car drivers were revered as heroes. The idolizing became even more intense as big-time race shops began springing up around the Charlotte area. There was more money in the pot and greater recognition for those in the big-league circuit.

So with that backdrop it should come as no surprise that women, looking for a way out of the mills, looked to the racetrack for a pass out of town. The first paragraph of *The Daily Independent* story reads: "Doris Roberts always dreamed of marrying a race car driver."

She bagged a keeper in May 1950, when Fireball Roberts, fresh from storming off the University of Florida campus to go racing for a living, showed up in town to compete at the old three-quarter mile Charlotte Speedway dirt track.

"As Doris remembers it," the story says, "Fireball kept coming over by her car to talk during a race and after it was over, the two joined friends for dinner."

In another version of the same tale, Doris, described by L. Spencer Riggs of *Automobile Quarterly*, as a "beautiful dark-haired girl" made herself very noticeable to Roberts at the track:

> Behind his pit area…, Doris was perched on the front fender of her car. From nearby Kannapolis, Doris and her older brother regularly attended racing events in the area.
>
> "I had seen Glenn drive at Daytona," Doris explained. "And now he'd come 'up country' to race against our boys."
>
> When Glenn walked around to get something out of his tow-car, he immediately noticed Doris. Striking up a conversation, he asked: "Who you pullin' for?"

"Now here is this guy, he's come up here and he's racing against my friends," Doris recalled. "So I said, 'I'm pulling for the winner.'"

"So he goes out and wins the first heat race," Doris continued.

When Glenn pulled into the pits he asked: "Well, who you pullin' for now?"

"The winner of the main event" replied the somewhat exasperated Doris. "He went out, missed all the wrecks and everything else and won the main event."

"Now, who are you pullin' for?" Glenn asked.

"Anybody can get lucky," came the quick replay.

Doris thought this was the end of her conversation with the brash racer. But her quick wit and beauty must have fascinated Glenn. Later, when he ran into her away from the track, he asked her out to dinner. At six foot two, looking like he was chiseled from stone, he was a formidable man.

"There were three girls with me," Doris explained. "I thought 'There's safety in numbers,' so I met him at the restaurant, I was so completely and utterly surprised at this man, that was so intelligent and unlike any race driver I had ever met, I really, really enjoyed dinner. He was the most unusual person to be driving a stock car.

"He never held a regular job," Doris maintains. "From 21 years of age, he was a professional race driver."

The Daily Independent: "After that it was a fast track all the way. The two married in York, South Carolina, a mere three weeks after they met and two weeks after he proposed."

They immediately set up house in Daytona Beach and within a year had a daughter, Pamela.

Roberts' best friend outside of racing was Bob Laney. They had raced together in the late 1940s as kids. When Glenn got back to Daytona as a married man, the first stop he made was to Laney's house. "I remember Glenn coming back from North Carolina after marrying Doris and he stopped on the way home," Laney said. " 'I got a surprise for you. I want you to meet my new wife Doris.' And I was like, 'Glenn, you what?' "

Maybe, as a precursor of things to come, Doris Roberts went back home to Kannapolis the last few months of her pregnancy to have the baby. She was young and didn't have a support system in Florida, and Fireball was constantly on the road, racing at short tracks in the South and throughout the country during the summer months.

After Doris delivered, the Robertses' relationship apparently morphed into a strange union of race car driver and somebody who wanted to be the wife of a race car driver. As time marched on, Mrs. Roberts was less and less a presence on the racing trail.

"Not for one moment has she regretted marrying Roberts," *The Daily Independent* story continues. "She was crazy about racing and madly in love with Glenn and they had some happy years together before the accident in Charlotte…"

In the *TDI* story Doris Roberts says, "You never really know someone before you marry them" and "We found each other. I wanted to be more than a spectator at the races, and we were immediately attracted to each other. I was a sport nut and racing was the sport of the area."

Their marriage officially lasted 14 years but soon after they were married, Fireball Roberts gained a reputation as a skirt-chasing, cavorting, party animal, who enjoyed late nights with good friends, alcoholic beverages and the company of wild women. That was the ultimate racer's life in those days, sort of a pirate on four wheels. "Doris and Glenn were never too happy." Bob Laney said.

In January, 1964, just four months before his divorce was finalized, Roberts granted *Sports Illustrated* an interview and played the part of a loving husband and caring father, which he was to Pamela. The scene was the living room of Roberts' house in Daytona Beach. The story reads:

> Fireball's wife Doris and his leggy 12-year-old, Pamela Jane, came into the living room. Doris drives a car well – Fireball pays her the great compliment of not wincing when she is at the wheel – and she is learning to fly, but does not hunt. "I went once," she said, "but never again. A duck fell on my head."

"Pammie, plug that in," Fireball said, pointing to a track with two model cars on the floor. "Now here's a tame way to race. This steering wheel controls it," he explained, and he and Pammie raced the models around the track. "I've lapped you four times, Dad," she observed. "I'm hung up, Pammie." He was, stalled sideways across the track.

"It's a toy that several race drivers endorsed," said Fireball. "I've only played with one of them. I raced [Freddie] Lorenzen on it, but he knew how, and I was just learning." Pressed, Fireball admitted with dignity that, no, he still was not the best man with the model cars. "His daddy can beat him," Pammie contributed helpfully.

The *Sports Illustrated* writer was female. She didn't completely fall for Roberts' living room play acting because she had followed the star racer on the circuit for a few races. She got a glimpse of the real Fireball Roberts but only offered hints of his genuine lifestyle in her five-page piece. By the way, that's the kind of space the magazine reserves only for the true superstars in any sport during any era.

The writer's first hint was quoting an unidentified novelist who said "I asked a kid who raced stock cars why he did it, and he told me he liked the life. Apparently, there are a lot of girls around, and he liked the idea of always being on the move and going and getting drunk."

Hmmm.

Apparently, she had followed Roberts and some of his racing buddies during a pre-race rite of passage because she reported a "whole-hearted, flat-out, simpleminded binge" by the group and likened the racing lifestyle to a "perennial college weekend."

More hints from the *Sports Illustrated* piece:

> (...Racers' parties have more the air of Roman orgies, if it is possible to imagine a Roman orgy punctuated with talk about fuel lines, engine blocks, exhaust pipes and gaskets. It should also be mentioned that Fireball – or "Fah-bawl, honey" as we say in these

circumstances – is a man people listen to even at an orgy. And a man, moreover, who, good and drunk, can compose ribald limericks, which may scan imperfectly but not without grace and devastating pertinence.)

One has to wonder why Doris Roberts put up with her husband's wanton ways. Hell, at times, she only tolerated her husband's racing pals. Pure Oil's Dick Dolan, who was a good friend of Roberts the last 10 years of his life, said "I knew Doris, but she wasn't particularly, well, let me put it this way, she wasn't overly friendly, although she knew I wasn't a bad influence on Glenn."

Most times that bad influence job was assigned to NASCAR's designated crazy men, Curtis Turner and Joe Weatherly, two memorable driving characters with whom Roberts had a strong association for many years; guilt by association in some cases. Turner and Weatherly won plenty of stock car races and never lost a party.

Maybe Doris Roberts knew from the beginning that Fireball's first love was made of metal, ran on tires and was capable of incredible speeds on a closed, walled circuit. When called to service as the perfect wife, she never missed a beat. She clung to this man like a ship-wrecked sailor clutches a life preserver in the middle of the Atlantic Ocean.

"She just wanted to be Mrs. Fireball Roberts," said somebody close to the situation. "That's all she ever wanted."

After Weatherly was killed at the start of the 1964 racing season, America's most famous race car driver took his daughter aside to ease her fears about his occupation. Weatherly, who had won back-to-back Grand National championships in 1962-63, died in a gruesome accident at Riverside, Calif., when his head struck a retaining wall. His car spun around, impacting the driver side of the car. Weatherly's head came through the side window and slammed against the concrete. He died instantly.

Roberts had a sitdown with Pamela in the days after Weatherly's

death. Roberts' true feelings were somewhat exposed. As told to the *Observer*, she said her father held his thumb and forefinger about an inch apart and said, "I love racing just this much more than I love you or your mother."

Fireball Roberts loved racing and had an insatiable appetite for the sport's lusty lifestyle and lived each day with complete and thorough gusto.

1956

33 Starts, 3 Poles
10 Races Led
5,695 Laps, 470 Laps Led
5 Wins, Rank: 7
Winnings: $14,742

Lockstep and Shadow

The year 1950 was not only big in Fireball Roberts' personal life – dropping out of college and taking a wife – it was also a racing linchpin which established the 21-year-old driver as a budding star in auto racing.

While he concentrated his efforts in the modified ranks – really old street cars cut up and tricked out to turn incredible laps on short, dirt ovals – Roberts made nine, patchwork Grand National starts, winning a pole position and a race at Occoneechee Speedway, a one-mile dirt oval in Hillsboro, North Carolina.

Before we go any further, a little history lesson is in order.

The primary racing machine of the day in the stock car ranks were the modified cars, which ran all sorts of combinations of car chassis and engines. On the old Daytona Beach & Road Course, for instance, they were the headline act from 1936 until 1949. There were no races during World War II.

After the war, William (Bill) H.G. France, who owned an Amoco gas station on Daytona's Main Street, got back into the race-promotion business, and realized the fledgling sport needed organization and continuity. Some of his counterparts in the promoting business in those days were sneaky bastards or just plain crooks. They would rent a fairgrounds track; advertise a race with a giant purse, then either sneak off during the race with the gate receipts or pay much less than the posted awards.

France called together every racing crony he knew for a stock car summit meeting on Dec. 14, 1947 in the Ebony Lounge high atop the Streamline Hotel in Daytona Beach. Among those at the table were Marshall Teague and Red Vogt, who both helped shape Roberts' racing career. They represented the mechanics' stake in a new organization and both would have a tremendous influence on young Fireball Roberts.

In the hall outside the meeting room were a number of younger participants, including Roberts and his future mechanical accomplice Speedy Spiers.

"There were a lot of unscrupulous promoters back then," Spiers said. "They said they would pay a certain amount of purse and after the race, they'd change the figure. They'd say, 'That's all I can pay you. We had a bad day at the ticket office.' That was one of the things NASCAR did that was good. They cleaned that up. That was the only good thing Bill France did. Don't get me wrong. He was a friend. He did some bad things to some people, but he was always good for me.

"Yeah, we was there for the first meeting at the Streamline. There were so many guys there, that Fireball and I was out in the hallway. We didn't sit down at the big table because we weren't important at the time."

Bill France Sr. was an imposing figure. He stood 6-foot-5 and had a deep, rumbling voice. He started out in the racing game as a mechanic and driver but turned his attention to promoting after moving to Florida from Washington, D.C., in 1935. Stock car racing was a helter-skelter affair in those days, with no clear-cut rules, and certainly no discipline.

France saw an opportunity to build a national sport and seized the moment. At the Streamline, he proposed a stock car governing board that would race by one set of rules, pay consistent purse money, offer injury protection to drivers and crown a national champion using a points formula.

Since he had the rights to one of stock car racing's largest annual shows at the Daytona Beach & Road Course, he carried a mighty big voice in the sport. France had the complete attention of his whiskey-drinking, cigarette-smoking counterparts, who were crammed around a black table in this dark, smoke-filled room, as he outlined his vision of the future.

"Nothing stands still in the world," he said in his opening remarks. "Things get better or worse, bigger or smaller."

Later he added: "Stock car racing has got distinct possibilities for Sunday shows. It would allow race-minded boys that work all week, who don't have the money to afford a regular racing car, to be competitive with a rich guy.

"There are a whole lot of things to be straightened out here. We've got to get track owners and promoters interested in building up stock car racing. I would like to get all of us in accord on as many different subjects as we can bring up.

"Right here within our group rests the outcome of stock car racing in the country today. We have the opportunity to set it up on a big scale."

The meetings lasted four days as the group roughed out technical rules, prize money disbursement, medical plans and a host of other subjects that would form a true stock car sanctioning body. They voted on a name and came up with the National Association for Stock Car Auto Racing or NASCAR for short.

After all these rules and regulations were committed to paper, France ran to his attorney, Louis Ossinsky Sr., and turned NASCAR into a private company and named himself president. France told Bill Tuthill, who was his right-hand man, that sanctioning bodies ruled by committee never worked because there was too much bickering among different interests.

"Just about the time the thing gets rolling, there is some dissidence; somebody gets irked and they vote the guy out of office that had done all the spadework," France had told Tuthill. "So we went to the lawyer and told him to set up the organization as a private corporation."

Once the seed was planted, up grew a mighty oak. France became known as a benevolent dictator, making all important calls "for the good of the sport" and leaving several unhappy folks in his wake. He had turned a very shaky sports alliance into a tangible family asset.

"If you knew France, it was, 'My way or no way,' " said Bob Laney. "I remember back when Bill France had a gas station on Main Street, and that was it. He was a sport. He had a lot of balls."

NASCAR began sanctioning races, mostly modifieds, in 1948. The following year France announced a new tour he called "Strictly Stock." These were passenger cars of the era with slight modifications for safety

reasons. The eight-race series was an instant success and quickly grabbed the attention of racing enthusiasts because the cars raced looked identical to those back in the family garage. Hell, they *were* the same cars back in the family garage.

Nobody knew it at the time, but France's NASCAR would become Fireball Roberts' playground. In turn, Roberts would develop into an important building block for France and help take stock car racing to a new level of acceptance. As a matter of fact, with his good looks, fan appeal and ability to speak, he became the face of NASCAR starting in 1958. He was the headline act, so to speak. NASCAR and Roberts were not just growing together, they were in complete lockstep.

A few years after Roberts' death, Darlington's public relations director Russ Catlin said Roberts made a lasting impression on the sport. Wrote Catlin about Roberts' impact: "When stock car racing completes its growing-up period, historians will discover that, like all other sports with a meager beginning, here and there along the line, some personality or happenstance came along to hasten and solidify the sport's growth."

Since Roberts and France lived in the same town, the young driver was fully aware of the NASCAR president's power and authority, which expanded with each passing season. Roberts never crossed France's train tracks or openly questioned his decisions. In 1961, when the Teamsters floated the idea of a "drivers' union," Roberts was first in, then bailed out, siding with the France family. His rationale? "It's the best thing goin'," Roberts said of NASCAR. "If you don't like it, don't drive." Said Laney: "When there was that strike, he didn't go with the guys who went on strike. There was some resentment."

Fireball Roberts had no time for politics. All this man did was race, race hard, and began building an undeniable fan base that stretched beyond the South's closed quarters.

With only one year under its belt, France made a bold decision to feature his "Strictly Stock" cars in a race at a new kind of speedway built in Darlington, S.C. The track, Darlington International Raceway, was a 1.25-mile paved oval, with banked turns. Harold Brasington, another man with a vision for the sport, built this track with his own hands on farming land about 10 miles from nowhere. It became a prototype course, an idea that others, including France, would borrow to build more racetracks with the same features – asphalt and banked turns.

France promoted the hell out of the race. Time trials lasted more than two weeks and 75 cars, with drivers from all over the country, showed up to participate. Johnny Mantz dubbed the "Madman" from Long Beach, California, started 43rd while Roberts, in an Oldsmobile, started 67th.

Mantz, who had Indianapolis racing experience, figured out that these big, heavy cars would wear out conventional tires quickly as they built heat and lost rubber by the chunk in the banked turns. He outfitted his 1950 Plymouth, partially owned by France, with tires that used a harder compound, much like the tires used on trucks in those days.

His strategy worked to perfection. Mantz just lumbered along as all the cars around him suffered one tire failure after another. Greg Fielden writes in his *Forty Years of Stock Car Racing*:

> The NASCAR boys did not know it, but they were in trouble. Red Byron, driving a Cadillac, ran 24 tires right off the rims while attempting to negotiate the high speed turns of Darlington...Mantz romped to a lopsided victory while watching most of his rivals retreat to the pit countless times for replacement of blown tires. His black fast-back Plymouth took the lead in the 50th lap and led the rest of the way, finishing nine laps ahead of Fireball Roberts.

The tire shortage that day had frenzied mechanics "borrowing" tires from spectator sedans parked in the infield. After the race, several fans were shocked to find their cars propped up on blocks, their wheels and tires "donated" to the racing effort. It was a wild and wooly afternoon that attracted an estimated 25,000 to this former peanut field.

Speedy Spiers was there to help Roberts in the pits and he scored the race differently than NASCAR. "I still think, to this day, that Fireball won the first Southern 500," Spiers said. "We used 32 tires for that race. We had eight or 10 laps on that Plymouth when we stopped for tires. That's another story. I still think we won that race, but we got paid for second." Again, no real argument from Roberts.

No matter. Roberts would return in his prime to win a couple of Southern 500s, a race that quickly became the benchmark in stock car racing. And by finishing second in 1950, he earned all sorts of championship points in this tour that France rechristened the Grand National Series.

A few weeks before Darlington, Roberts had scored his first Grand National win at Occoneechee, and went into the season finale at the same track in contention to earn national championship honors. It was the 19th and final race of the season.

According to Fielden, in his detailed *Forty Years of Stock Car Racing, Volume I*, all Roberts needed to do was back off throttle and secure fifth place to steal the title from Bill Rexford, who had entered 17 races that season, eight more than Roberts. But backing off the gas was not the Fireball way.

Fielden writes: "Fireball Roberts had an opportunity to take the title with a fifth-place finish after Rexford had succumbed to engine problems early in the race. Instead of employing a conservative effort in order to take the championship, Roberts opted to charge hard all day. His reasoning was that the race paid $1,500 to win and the championship was worth $1,000."

Remember, he was 21, had a pregnant wife at home and bills to pay. Bill Gazaway raced against Roberts in those days and prize money was critical to make the next show. "The old times," Gazaway said, "was the lean times. We didn't have time to socialize like they do today. You raced, then hooked up to the tow car and pulled it someplace else. Everything was lean back then."

The $500 difference was enough for Roberts to keep his foot in the throttle. At that moment in his life, the money was more important

than the title trophy from a two-year-old series. He mashed the gas and went for the race victory. It cost him. On lap 126 of the 175 scheduled that day, the engine expired and Roberts finished 21st.

"Which one did you think I'd go after?" Roberts told a writer after being asked about the difference in money. Said Doris to *Automobile Quarterly*: "Glenn never cared about championships. He went out there to win."

Rexford, from Findlay Park, New York, won the 1950 championship honors. Rexford was an aberration in stock car racing. His lone Grand National victory came in his championship season. Rexford never finished in the top 10 in points again and dropped out of sight following the '52 season. Still, he and Mantz had served a purpose for France. The guy who won the biggest race of the year was from California. The driver who captured the championship hailed from the Empire State. Rexford and Mantz showed that NASCAR was being noticed by people outside the Southern sphere.

In comparison to Rexford, Roberts was just beginning a stellar NASCAR career, although he only saw spot duty in Grand National racing for the next five years preferring to concentrate his efforts in the modified ranks. Roberts didn't win another Grand National event until 1956, mostly because he wasn't really trying.

When he got to the big show, he became the big show.

1957
42 Starts, 4 Poles
16 Races Led
6,891 Laps, 1,107 Laps Led
8 Wins, Rank: 6
Winnings: $19,829

No Stupid Questions

By now you may have summarized Edward Glenn Roberts, Jr. as one bad-assed, single-minded, money-grubbing, heartless prick who cared only about himself, running fast, winning races at any cost and bedding another woman as fast as the sun would set.

And, in a sense, you would be right because when it came to racing, when he was in full Fireball persona, Roberts was all those things and more. At the racetrack, he had the blinders on – his complete focus on the car, the race, the task at hand. Inside his racing machine, he had tunnel vision, but was fully sensitized to his surroundings.

At any given moment during a race, he could tell you: what lap it was, where he was in the running order, how much gas was in the tank, if his oil pressure was OK, who was running in front of him, who was nudging him from behind, who he had pissed off and how the car was handling in different parts of the track. He was like a computer with size 12 shoes.

With all these things flying around in his head, Roberts was especially unfriendly before making a time trial run which separated the men racers from the squeaky boys in speed toys. Back in those days, before there were engineers and computers, $600 race tires and exotic race setups, only the bravest men would push their stock car equipment to its limit, or beyond, to earn top qualifying honors at the emerging superspeedway racetracks.

HE'S ON THE POLE AGAIN

Fireball: 'Qualifying High Takes the Most Guts'

BY BILL ROBINSON

FRED LORENZEN (L) SITS IN SECOND SLOT
Bobby Johns (R) Is Sixth With 138.910

FAMILIAR SPOT FOR FABULOUS FIREBALL
Roberts Grabs Pole Post With Record Run

"We're always running right on that ragged edge," Roberts groused to an Atlanta newspaper reporter in 1962. "It takes more guts to qualify high than to win a race.

"Qualifying is a battle of balance, a battle of wits and a battle of guts. Maybe that's why I get more kicks from it than anything in the racing game. In a race, anything can happen. Qualifying is the only true test of a man and machine against others. I really and truly think the good qualifiers stick their necks out a little bit more than the others most of the time."

This was serious dealings. So, when he was in race driver mode, he wasn't in the mood to talk, socialize, share a joke or take visual measurements of scantly-clad trophy queens. His mind was filled to the brim with business details, which included things like carburetor settings, sway bar and spring selection, and weather and track conditions. In other words, when he was milling around the racetrack garage, hovering around his car, he was in his office trying to close a deal, get a contract, advance his career. He had no time for, well, dumb nonsense bullshit. It was a good time to get the hell out of the way and leave the man alone.

"He wasn't a nice guy," says Greg Fielden. "He was a professional."

Judy Judge said Roberts had multiple personalities. At the racetrack, he used a Southern twang, shared a laugh or two with competitors, but could get grumpy as hell with the media or other hangers-on.

"When he was with them, the racers, that's what he was," Judge said. "When he wasn't with them, he wasn't like that. He was two or three different people. When he was focused on racing, he was focused on racing. Don't ask him a stupid question like, 'What happened?'

He'd say, 'I don't know. Why are you asking me dumb things like that?' When he was out, he was an entirely different man. He would and could talk to anybody about anything. He was a chameleon."

A very popular lizard, not only with men who appreciated the sport of racing, but with the ladies, who thought he was an all-man wonder.

"In his day, he was popular or famous or a celebrity, whatever you want to call it," said JoAnne, Roberts' sister. "I think he handled it quite well. It didn't seem to bother him. I think he relished it. I don't think the spotlight bothered him. There were places and times where he wanted his privacy and didn't want to be bothered. If he was bothered, he would let you know."

Tim Sullivan, who served in many racing capacities over the years, said Buck Baker, a two-time Grand National Series champion, would greet Roberts in the garage area by saying "Hi motherfucker."

"Weatherly and Turner called Fireball, 'Mr. Son of a Bitch,'" Sullivan added with a hoot.

Roberts certainly wasn't a favorite of the media, which grew in numbers as the series gained recognition in the late 1950s and early '60s. PR man Russ Catlin writes:

> To face facts, Fireball Roberts did not have a good "press" during his career. His victories had to be reported, but all too often his short answers, if he did answer at all, and his dislike of playing phony with anyone, won him few "most popular" awards among the writing gentry. In conversation and in print he has been described as moody, selfish, egotistical, rude, self-

centered and money-hungry.

All of that was true – to varying degrees – depending on one's own interpretation of life."

Yes, at the racetrack, in the hours leading up to events, and during races and immediately following some of these white-knuckle speed battles, yes, Fireball Roberts was a no good dick with ears with nothing nice to say about nothing. The absolute worst place to hold a conversation with Roberts was at the racetrack, surrounded by a sea of race cars, because he took his job, took his profession, quite seriously.

"He was a sort of taciturn person; he didn't have a lot to say," Lowe's Motor Speedway president Humpy Wheeler said. "I myself think he was a little shy. I think that's what it really was. He wasn't aloof, he was just shy. That was a common trait among a lot of drivers at the time. At the same time, you knew he was a self-confident person behind the steering wheel, you could just tell that; but he didn't talk a lot."

Pure Oil's Dick Dolan said Roberts was NASCAR's first truly professional driver, and Roberts had the documents to prove it. "It said so on his driver's license," Dolan said. "When he filled out applications, when it asked for occupation, he always put down 'professional race car driver' long before anybody else did. You have to remember the era, you know, some cops were always trying to put race drivers in jail when they caught 'em speeding. He was proud of being a good race car driver. So, that's what he put on his driver's license, and he's the only one that I know of, and I've known an awful lot of racers, that actually claimed that racing was their occupation."

If a member of the media asked NASCAR's first pro driver a stupid question, they got an earful of jawing from the apparent quick-tempered, asphalt warrior.

"He didn't get along very good with the press," Speedy Spiers said. "They'd ask Fireball some dumb question and he'd tell them what he thought of it. One time he blew an engine in a qualifying race and there was oil smoke everywhere. Somebody stuck a microphone in his face and he batted it away. The reporter asked him 'What happened Fireball?' He said 'You dumb son of a bitch, don't you have eyes? Did you think I started a campfire out there with all this smoke?' That kind of stuff didn't endear him to the press."

Chris Economaki, racing's revered Yoda-like racing editor and publisher, said he had a very short, terse conversation with Roberts about television and the racing workplace. Economaki, now well into his 80s, is the dean of American motorsports journalism and for years moonlighted as a racing television reporter.

"I can tell you this, in the early days of television, he came to me and he said, 'Chris, don't come around me with that microphone," Economaki said. " 'We can't touch those Hemis (Chrysler's powerful V8 engine). They got our back to the wall I'm not gonna talk on television.' That was interesting to me."

The members of the press, who didn't take the time or make the effort to know the entire Fireball Roberts, only saw one side, mostly the grumpy or aloof appearing driver. They didn't bother to get the panoramic, 360-degree reading on this most unique individual. Roberts was not a normal man and certainly not your everyday stock car driver. There were many sides and levels to this guy who drove a stock car for a living. Actually, there were two sides of Roberts on almost every issue that impacted his life.

Think about it: he had asthma but smoked and worked out; he

had a wife and kid but acted like a swinging bachelor; he was kind of a sickly child and became one of America's most celebrated athletes; he hated Daytona Beach when he first moved there but made the honky-tonk beach town his home as an adult; he was married but had a steady girlfriend. The list goes on and on.

There were only a handful of media that actually went out of their way to discover the true Fireball, scan the entire Roberts package. One of those was Max Muhleman, who served as the auto racing writer for the *Charlotte News*. Muhleman first met Roberts at a Darlington media gathering in 1958.

"When I went to the races, I never got expenses or anything," Muhleman said. "That was unheard of in those days. I guess that's one reason there weren't many of us out there. We were in the old Darlington pagoda, which was in the infield at the end of the pits. It was the size of a closet. We were up there talking after qualifying. I asked him some sort of question or two. He just seemed to have a whole lot more in his head than just racing to me."

So to shake things up, to get a reaction and reading, Muhleman asked Roberts an off-the-wall question to see how the driver would respond.

"I said something like, 'Did you ever think about running around this track on foot?' You ask that to most stock car drivers, particularly guys back then, and they would look at you sideways and call security. Fireball just chuckled. He said, 'It would probably take me 20 minutes to do that.' I said, 'It wouldn't take you 20 minutes. I bet you I could do it under 10.' He told me I couldn't do it under 10. This is the least likely conversation you could ever have with a stock car driver. He said, 'I'll bet you a steak dinner you can't run this track in under 10 minutes.' I told him, 'I'm gonna go right now. Let me go find some tennis shoes.'

"He started laughing and called me back and said, 'Anybody that would try that deserves a steak dinner.' So we went to dinner that night. We talked about racing about 25 percent of the time and about things he liked to do and current affairs. He was a renaissance man. He had a wide appetite and interest in life. I found that fascinating."

In a sport where most of the participants were lucky to have a complete high school education, or boast a complete set of teeth, Muhleman had found a cultural diamond in a vast pit of coal.

Muhleman, unlike a majority of his pencil and notepad toting counterparts, almost immediately got the full measure of Edward Glenn Roberts Jr. Muhleman kept digging through that mine for the next six years and was one of the very few people who had pieced together the entire Fireball jigsaw puzzle, and had planned to write a book about this driver.

"If you talked to Fireball one on one in a conversational way, it was certainly easier to talk to him," he said. "We hit it off. We formed a friendship.

"He had that sort of aloofness but I think it was because he was organized and wanted to get from point 'A' to point 'B.' He kept schedules. He had his act together in a before-his-time sort of way.

"He cared about life in a big way. He was very intelligent. Read a lot. He could talk about religion and politics and talk at depth and so eloquently. He could carry on polite arguments. He was a renaissance man for his time, for any time."

Bob Meyers had the benefit of riding Muhleman's coattails when it came to approaching Roberts, but had his own impression of the driver. "He was kind of an unusual guy around the racetrack; a lot of people thought he was aloof and didn't want to talk to anybody," he said. "I learned from knowing him that a lot of that was just his concentration on his car, and he didn't like any nonsense going on around him."

Thanks to Muhleman, Meyers was able to see the sum of the man, not just the racetrack fraction. Roberts even went out of his way to help Meyers once. "I had had a pretty rough night before and I didn't feel good the next morning – OK, I was hung over – so I told Max, 'Go ahead to the race and I'll catch up to you.' When I started to the racetrack, there was so much darn traffic that I turned around and went back to the motel. Max wanted me to do a story on the second-place driver that day. We call that a sidebar. Anyway, to make a long story short, Fireball, finished second and came to the motel where I was staying. I interviewed him and got the story Max wanted me to do. It was easier than if I had gone to the racetrack."

Judy Judge said Muhleman was one of about three people that Roberts truly trusted, even though Max "stole" one of his racing uniforms.

"One time Max got into Glenn's uniform after a rainout day, I think it was Atlanta, and he was downstairs in the lobby of the motel signing autographs as Fireball Roberts," she said. "It was hysterical. The driver suit was way too big for him."

"Glenn and Max were very different people, but they hit it off so well," she continued. "They just had fun together and Glenn trusted him with things he told him. Max never let him down. If you disappointed Glenn, like told him you would do something but didn't do it, you were off his list after that. If he couldn't count on you, you were not going to be around, period. When he cut somebody out, he cut them out for the rest of his life."

As a competitor, Roberts was tougher than the tip of a jackhammer. Away from the racetrack, he might have been one of the most fun-loving humans ever to walk the earth. Yes, he would frequent those completely out of control Turner-Weatherly shindigs, which involved loud music, whiskey, women, nudity and the occasional live animal (Weatherly once coaxed a live mule, for reasons unknown, into a second-floor motel party room using a broomstick). Other times, he would just hang out at one of his favorite bars or restaurants around Daytona Beach. He had a close-knit circle of friends, who simply adored being around his quick wit and monster laugh.

"He loved to go out and drink," Judge said. "He would write hysterical limericks. He and Max would write limericks on a table cloth that would have the people at tables around them laughing."

"When we went out at night, he wanted to go where the fun was, where it was bright and loud, and we did. He was very bright and charming. He never stayed where there was trouble. When he saw it coming, he was gone."

Dick Dolan and Roberts were about the same age when they first met in 1954. They had a professional relationship at the racetrack and were friends once the track gates swung closed and locked for the day.

"We struck it off pretty good together," Dolan said. "We both played a little golf at a time when race drivers didn't play golf. They never had time for that kind of thing. We were the terror on Seabreeze Boulevard (lined with restaurants and bars). At this bar called the 19th Hole, there was a bowling machine in there and he and I were probably the top players in the place. When we would team up together, we could beat anybody in town.

"You know, people would say, 'He's kind of cool to people.' And, he was, until you got to know him a little. Until you got to know him, he was kind of reserved. We were both scotch-and-water drinkers. He would get a few belts in him and so would I and we'd be pretty friendly with everybody. I really don't remember how I got to be close to him other than we were the same age and we golfed a little bit and went hunting. I guess we had a little bit in common."

Roberts was cocksure. No question there. Sometimes, Roberts would challenge people to a game at the 19th Hole bowling game and use one of his stocking feet instead of his hand. A race driver with a swagger and strut knows he belongs in the game and ahead of the pack. But in ordinary circumstance on an average day, he was just Glenn Jr. to folks who knew him around this resort town. "If you know somebody before they become famous, like I knew Glenn, to me, he was just a friend of mine," Bob Laney said. "We'd do anything for each other. We were just good buddies."

"He was just a laid-back guy from Daytona Beach," says Richard Petty, a seven-time NASCAR champion. "Yeah, he loved to drive a race car, but he loved life. He was pretty wide open. He was friendly with fans, but he was different. He had a more wild life than I did. He was out partying and doing that deal. But when it got serious, he could get really serious with it, too."

Roberts made enough money to live anywhere in the country, but he chose to stay in Daytona Beach because of its gaudy, party atmosphere. "I've got it made just staying home and enjoying it," he said once. "Thousands and thousands of people save up all year just to spend a week or two here."

Roberts did mix business and pleasure sometimes at the track. He would love to take civilians (non-race car drivers) in rides at NASCAR's big tracks. His favorite joy-riding arena was Daytona International Speedway. He took Tim Sullivan for a spin – once. "Yeah, he took me down the backstretch in a Pontiac race car that was equipped with a camera to shoot some movie," Sullivan said. "I'm sitting there in this little seat and he looks over at me and says, 'This old things runs pretty good at 170 mph, doesn't it?' Then he gets into Turn 3 and lets go of the steering wheel. I about shit my pants."

Life, as you know, isn't all green grass, a bowl of cherries, a soft spring breeze, a day at the beach, the laughter of children, a new puppy, an IRS refund; or getting off work early, a freshly waxed car, a wrinkle-free blouse, a competent babysitter, your wedding day, a five-day cruise to the Bahamas, an afternoon at the spa and a day without having to cook.

Life, as we know it, has its ups and downs, and peaks and valleys. It can be exciting one day, mundane the next, sad, frustrating, irritating, exhilarating, happy, routine, disturbing, frightening, and joyful. You name it.

Fireball Roberts may have been a Superman-like figure to some, but he was still a human, chock full of emotions like any other man or woman. He just didn't show it in public much. After losing the 1961 Daytona 500 in the closing laps, he was lower than toenail fungus because that was the one race that fate kept prying from his strong grip.

Tom Brown, of the *Daytona Beach Morning Journal*, captured the moment in ink:

> The great racing machines roared by monotonously, clicking off the anticlimactic final laps of the Daytona 500. Fireball Roberts didn't see them.
>
> Roberts sat on a stack of tires in his nearly deserted pit sobbing in frustration and anger.
>
> Somebody shoved a paper cup of water into his hands but nobody spoke to him. His grief was too deep, his agony wrenching him apart.
>
> Roberts had just seen his latest bid for victory in "the big one" vanish only 13 laps from victory lane.
>
> Smokey Yunick, pit chief and builder of Roberts'

Pontiac, finally placed an arm around his shoulder and muttered sympathy.

When they were gone from the pit, Roberts rose to his feet and with a deep curse hurled the crumpled cup to the ground.

Later, as Marvin Panch accepted the winner's plaudits, Roberts began to talk, hesitatingly, not trusting a voice obviously chocked with emotion.

"I can't win here," he said. "I just can't win a big one here. The only big race I ever won in Daytona was on the beach – and they took that one away from me. What the hell's with this place that I can't win here?"

To win the Daytona 500 has become a consuming passion with Roberts, and, understandably. Aside from the gold and glory involved, the Daytona ace would like to show the homefolks – just once.

"The best car, the best mechanic and pit crew, just coasting along – and then bang. It's all shot to hell. A whole year's planning and work and expense."

"The thing that really gets me," he continued, "is that not once all afternoon did I have to punish the car. Not once did I put my foot in it all the way around. It was just a nice easy ride.

"And then a screwball thing like that starter coming loose happens. Why?"

A kid shoved a program and a pen at Roberts for his autograph. Fireball looked at him a moment then said softly: "Not now, son. I don't feel much like writing right now. Maybe I'll feel like it in a few minutes."

As he matured, it was harder for him to contain all those things that stir up in one's emotional pot. Once, as they sat in his car at the beach, Judge says Roberts talked about a health concern of a family member then "cried like a baby."

"He was a very sensitive man," she said of her famous fiancé. "Most people didn't see that side of him."

1958

10 Starts, 0 Poles

7 Races Led

2,491 Laps, 877 Laps Led

6 Wins, Rank: 11

Winnings: $32,219

Fish in the Halifax

Fireball Roberts liked to go fast, and even with the growing popularity of Bill France's Grand National Series, the young driver preferred the raw speed and intense competition offered in the modified ranks as the 1950s marched forward. The Grand National machines were slow and awkward, just the opposite of the nimble, horsepower-rich mods.

"I started racing for a living in 1950," Roberts told *Sports Illustrated* in '64. "Until 1956, for six years, my education in racing was in modified stock cars."

Between 1950 and '55, Roberts competed in only 34 of the 213 Grand National events staged by NASCAR. He didn't have an exceptional record in that class. If you dismiss the 1950 GN season, Roberts produced only six top-10 finishes and had no top-five finishes between 1952-55. He didn't have the greatest equipment or interest to compete at that level. When he entered a Grand National race, he was doing somebody a favor or looking to pick up some extra money.

After a close second-place finish in the final 1950 standings, Roberts was ranked 201st by NASCAR in '55, making just two starts over the length of the 45-race schedule. In his first start of the season, over the Daytona Beach & Road Course, Roberts led all the laps, won the race but was later disqualified for a technical infraction. Roberts had made mention of this bad day after he fell out of the '61 Daytona 500, while leading with a little more than a dozen laps left.

Ray Fox and Red Vogt, both from Daytona Beach, were legendary racing mechanics in the making in 1955. They had collaborated  to enter a car for their boss Bob Fish, who owned Fish Carburetor Corporation. Fox, Vogt and Roberts all worked for Bob Fish in the early 1950s. Vogt was responsible for the chassis, Fox the motor.

"He (Fish) sponsored Fireball in his early career," Fox told racing journalist Bob Moore. "He was just a kid back then. But it didn't take long to see that he was one helluva driver. Fireball was also a real engineer. He really knew what it took to make a race car run fast."

Fox said Fish decided to enter a Buick, with Roberts behind the wheel, in one of those 11th-hour, what-the-hell kind of situations. Fox started to piece a race engine together the night before the race. He would later become famous for these late-night mechanical heroics.

"I started at 8 p.m. and didn't finish until 4 a.m.," Fox told Moore. "And they wouldn't let us use one of Mr. Fish's carburetors. So we had to use one from K-Mart."

L. Spencer Riggs in *Automobile Quarterly* picks up the story from here:

> Since it was in his hometown, Fireball always strived to win the grueling 160-mile contest. But his cars seldom stood the test. His eighth-place finish in '54 had been his high water GN mark.
>
> For the '55 event, Roberts landed a ride in the Bob Fish Carburetor Buick, wrenched by legendary mechanic Red Vogt. During practice, Fireball learned the big nailhead had the power he needed. Tim Flock's Chrysler 300 took the pole at a sensational 130.29 mph, with Lee Petty's Chrysler second at 127.11 and Dick Rathmann's Olds third at 122.24. Not wanting to tip his hand, Roberts took fourth at 121.11. When the green flag flew on race day, Fireball vaulted into the lead and started to pull away from the field. But with only five of 39 laps completed, he was nearly asphyxiated by exhaust fumes. Discovering he was suddenly woozy, he rolled down all the windows as he roared around the course. At the end of ten laps, he had a 25-second lead on Tim Flock. It wasn't long before his pursuers had given up any hope of catching the big Buick being thrown into slides hundreds of feet up the beach, negotiating the turn onto the paved highway. Roberts took the checkered flag with a 74-second advantage over time Flock, with Petty third.
>
> But when the Fish Buick was inspected, it was discovered the pushrods had been shortened .032 of an inch...NASCAR rules called for absolutely no modifications from stock production engines. So on Monday afternoon following the Sunday race,

NASCAR commissioner E.G. "Cannonball" Baker declared Roberts disqualified, giving the victory to Tim Flock.

"It [shortening the pushrods] didn't alter the speed or performance of the engine," Roberts maintained. "I never knew anything about the engine, until last night after the race."

"We shortened the pushrods to allow for a thin head gasket officials said we could use," Vogt explained. "I was as surprised as anybody."

"We won the race, but they disqualified us," Fox says today. "I did win a race on the old beach course, but I didn't get credit for it." Then adding with a laugh, "NASCAR was bad, bad, bad." Fox worked for NASCAR in the 1990s.

In terms of earning enough money to support a family, Roberts did OK, because he had a fairly sweet deal with Fish, who manufactured aftermarket carburetors. Fish started his little company in Massachusetts then relocated to Florida to escape the harsh winters. The company was based in Daytona Beach, just off the Seabreeze Boulevard Bridge on the mainland side of the city.

Fish, who had no formal engineer's schooling, offered several different makes of carburetors, some that got better gas mileage than the factory models, and many that produced more horsepower and more speed. Roberts had two jobs with Fish. He worked at the shop as an engineer and mechanic, and in the spring and summer he would race modifieds outfitted with Fish Carburetors.

In "The Fish Carburetor Story" on the www.fireballroberts.com Web site, Daytona Beach racing historian Roland Via writes: "The 'Fish' was seen as a very serious threat to the 'Original Equipment' establishment and could not be tolerated. He [Fish] suffered years of dirty tricks and persecution in an attempt to put him and his carburetor out of business. He even had his mail stopped on trumped-up charges which were entirely untrue and the case never went to court. It was simply a deliberate time-wasting exercise to stop his cash flow and ruin him. He was not to be beaten and moved to Florida where he kept going by selling carbs to individuals, including some wealthy big game fishermen which enabled them to reach and return from their fishing grounds much quicker…"

Fielding his own modified team was the perfect way to spread the word on Fish products to automobile enthusiasts because, unlike the Grand National Series, the modified class offered lots of leeway for race car modifications (ergo, the modified moniker).

It was here, working at Fish Carburetor and racing the "M-1" modified car, that the name of Edward Glenn Roberts Jr., "Fireball" to be specific, was beginning to circulate to hard-core race fans and big shots in the auto industry.

"We worked together a long time," says Fox, now in his 80s. "We worked together for Mr. Fish for many, many years. He and I helped build all the carbs, all the racing carbs." The Halifax River, which ran behind the shop, became a watery grave for many of the prototype carburetors that failed to meet Fish expectations. Roberts made good use of his throwing arm. While he did spend time in the shop (sometimes Fox would catch him sleeping at his desk), Roberts' primary duty was to run the wheels off race cars and prove the Fish carburetor's worth.

"He got paid from Fish and while he worked for them, he made pretty good money and he was able to have whatever cars he wanted," Fox said. "I remember one time we built a Cadillac engine and put it in a Ford modified car."

Those were some interesting times, as Roberts and his mechanic Speedy Spiers towed modifieds from their Florida-based camp to every little crappy-ass, dust-bowl track from the Carolinas to New York through the Midwest.

"I started to build cars and he drove my cars for a couple of years, then we went to work at Fish Carburetor and I traveled with him with the Fish cars," Spiers said. "We raced their cars all over the place. We traveled together for about three years. We campaigned all over the place with our two little old race cars that we had on our own."

It was in these super-fast machines on those no-name dirt tracks that Fireball Roberts experienced and learned the racing game inside and out, where he honed his skill as a "professional race car driver." He raced in NASCAR sanctioned events and in other series scattered across the country. To this day, modified racing is a patchwork of regional sanctioning bodies, racing under different rules and configurations.

In the 1950s, modified racing was wide-open and hell bent. With the right planning and a sturdy mechanic, a driver could race almost every night of the week. Racers would bumper-tow their racing machines behind a passenger car. If times got tough, the passenger car could be used as a racer.

This sort of racing was hardly high society. Roberts competed against some of the meanest and nastiest drivers in the sport's history. Since he was the "out of town" driver, the local promoter would cast favor on his regulars. Most of the time, Roberts had to start from the rear of the field because of his hometown listing, not the strength of his race car. It was in these formative years that the Fireball name, bestowed for his baseball throwing abilities, transferred to his racing expertise and style.

"He was a fierce competitor," Speedy Spiers says today. "He was one of them guys you had to slow down, not one you had to speed up. He was that good of a driver. You had to keep the brakes on him because he was tearing equipment up so bad. The equipment we had really wasn't that good, so he would save it in qualifying and use it up in the race. He'd come charging up through the pack and somebody would get in his way and he'd shorten their car up about three feet, and his, too. I told him, 'Hey man, you can't win the race on the first lap.'

"I told him running over people don't win races and don't make friends either. I told him pretty soon they would be talking to him behind the grandstand – three or four of them, with wrenches in their hands. Well, 'pretty soon' never happened. Most of those races back then were 25 or 30 laps. I'd tell him to wait a bit and let it string out a little, then start passing cars. He finally got better. We finally got to the point where we'd get appearance money. You couldn't make it on prize money. You couldn't stay on the road with prize money even if you won every race you went to. When he got good enough to get appearance money, we did pretty good and won quite a few races. We'd go up to New York State or whatever and spend the whole summer there and come back to Florida and race here in the winter."

Speedy Spiers, now in his 70s, remembers that magic moment when a promoter closed the door to his office, and started talking with greenbacks in hand. The first time it happened was in Chicago, not what you call a bastion of stock car racing even in today's world. Andy Granitelli, who would become famous for kissing Mario Andretti on the lips after his STP-sponsored car won the Indianapolis 500, started out in racing as a promoter. He was one of those independents who worked out of his hat.

"Andy Granitelli leased out Soldier's Field in Chicago and would run races," Spiers recalled. "He was really good to us. He gave us really good appearance money. He called us the 'Alligators' because we lived in Florida. Fireball had a hard time winning races like that because the local guys with the points would start up front. We had no points.

When you start last among 40 cars on a football field, well, that's a mess to get through. We'd always start on the tail and the best we could ever finish was fifth I think.

"Tom Pistone won most of those Chicago races back then. He lived there, had good equipment and started on the pole every week. But Granitelli treated us really good. He gave us $1,500 one night and we thought it was the end of the world. That was big money in the 1950s. We finished fifth and after the race, he kept counting out money and there was $1,500 in Fireball's hand. He said, 'I want you to come back next week.' Fireball said, 'Hell, we ain't gonna go back to Florida for this kind of money. They pay you here.' "

Roberts and Spiers raced as a tag-team, driving duo when they first started out on the modified circuit, but Spiers soon gave up the steering wheel to concentrate on Roberts' cars. Why? Because Spiers survived one horrific accident at a short track in Fayetteville, North Carolina, and said adios to the driving.

"I don't remember it, but my car started to flip end over end and I tore down about 100 feet of wood fence," Spiers said. "I ended up in the hospital. No more racing for me. Fireball kept telling me, 'Man, you got more ability than anybody I've seen.' I told him, 'You keep telling me that and you are going to get me killed. I'll let you do the driving and I'll work on the cars.' That's the way it was from then on. I kept his stuff up a long time."

There is no performance chart to show Roberts' sterling modified record, but his feature victories can be easily counted by the hundreds. And the people who watched him, well, they knew he was some kind of talent.

"When he started driving, boy he was a sight!" said Rev. Hal Marchman, who has said the pre-race prayers at Daytona International Speedway since 1960. "Big Bill" France offered up the racing blessing when the track opened in 1959 and ended his prayer with "Sincerely, Bill France." From then on, Marchman was handed the microphone, to say a blessing for the men who climbed into those incredibly fast machines.

"In those days, drivers won the races," Chris Economaki says. "Today I'm sure, you all know, cars win the races. The technology wasn't there that prevails today. So people knew it was the man that won the race; the car wasn't of significance."

While his modified record is not completely known, Roberts would tell people that he led almost every race he started, a trait that carried over to his Grand National Series career, and gained him favor in board rooms and bedrooms, across the country.

1959
8 Starts, 3 Poles
3 Races Led
1,445 Laps, 147 Laps Led
1 Win, Rank: 16
Winnings: $10,865

A Man's Man

"Glenn and I were," Bob Laney says, "the world's greatest duck hunters."

That wasn't some kind of inside code for chasing women and having sex. Fireball Roberts was an accomplished duck hunter and Laney was the guy who first showed him how to be a sportsman. Well, and of course, as Laney says, "We had one or two beers along the way."

Other than gaining volumes of carnal knowledge through the 1950s, Roberts enjoyed playing golf, pool, amateur jai-alai and duck hunting to relax and unwind from the stress of driving race cars.

Obviously, legends grow with the passing of time, much like a dune builds from blowing sand, but people of good faith and reason and solid mental capability, insist to this day that Fireball could have beat "Fast" Eddie Felson or Minnesota Fats – with one hand tucked in a back pocket.

That skinny little ol' nothing of a boy, who stayed indoors a lot because of his asthma, turned out to be one helluva athlete, excelling in activities that required hand-eye coordination.

Speedy Spiers to this day, more than 40 years after last seeing his friend, cannot believe the reach of Roberts' athletic prowess. "Yeah, he was a natural driving an automobile," he said. "That's a natural talent I guess, but he was athletic even though he had asthma. He'd climb the damn palm trees like a monkey. He would put his arms around the palm tree and put his feet right up against the tree and climb up there like nothing. Have you ever seen anybody do that before? Me neither."

Roberts put that God-given ability to good use by learning to play 8-ball and 9-ball as a teen-ager. He moved from pool hall to pool hall until finding a home at Frank's Newsstand, which was on the corner of Main Street and Grandview Avenue in Daytona's beachside.

"Frank's was his primary hangout as a teen-ager," his sister JoAnne said. "He used to play for money, too." Legend has it he earned enough money hustling pool to pay for gas and performance parts for that car that JoAnne hated to drive.

Jai-alai, pronounced *high lie*, was imported to this country from the Basque region of Spain. It became a legal pari-mutuel game in Florida and Connecticut. What the hell is it? Jai-alai is a court game somewhat like handball played on a three-wall court by two or four players with a ball and a long curved wicker basket strapped to the wrist. The players catch a very hard rubber ball (pelota) with the long basket (cesta) and hurl it at the front wall at speeds approaching 150 mph. In other words, this was no game for the pussycats among us.

When he wasn't on the court playing as an amateur at the Daytona Beach Jai-Alai Fronton, he was in the stands placing bets. "He had a system, you know," Judge says. "He always bet the same numbers."

Oh, the advantages of living in a resort town, where Roberts experienced the high-life in nightclubs, pari-mutuel facilities, golf courses and in the wild on a regular basis.

Duck hunting may have been his favorite pastime. During the

winter, Roberts and his gang would drink all night then head south to Brevard County to shoot ducks.

"We'd go where the launching pads are now at Cape Canaveral," Laney said. "There was a big lagoon down there, Mosquito Lagoon. They dug a canal from the north end of the lagoon to the Banana River. They call that Haulover Canal because before it was dug, they had to haul the boats over from lagoon to the river. During the winter, we'd have tremendous duck populations. We used to go down there and duck hunt all the time. He won a 10-horsepower motor in some contest. We'd take that Mercury motor and rent a boat.

L. To R,
DicK DOLAN, RACING DIR.
FOR PUROIL
NELSON STACY.
FIREBALL ROBERTS
+ RUSTY, A DOG BY TRADE
DUCK HUNTING
ALLENHURST FISH CAMP
ON HAULOVER
(GOT THE LIMIT) (WED & THURS)

"We'd party up until 2 or 3 o'clock in the morning, then go home and change clothes, you know, put on our waders, and go down to Haulover where there was a fishing camp. We'd go down and get a boat and hang a motor on it and go duck hunting until 9 or 10."

Dick Dolan went on several duck outings with Roberts & Co. They were joined at various times by Nelson Stacy, another local racer, and Tiny Lund, who stood 6-foot-5 in bare feet. Lund won the 1963 Daytona 500, subbing for Marvin Panch, who was burned in a sportscar accident in the weeks leading up to the big race. Panch, if you remember, won the 1961 Daytona 500 after Roberts dropped out with mechanical problems. At the track, these guys were like tigers battling over a fat wilderbeast. Away from the track, they resembled frat brothers on a weekend outing.

"We loved hunting," Dolan said. "We'd go duck hunting, Fireball and Nelson and I. 'Member Stacy? He used to live over there on White Street and he was a tank driver during the war. Tough guy, but a nice guy. I mean really tough as nails. We were duck hunting the day NASA shot the monkey into space at Cape Canaveral. The rocket went right over our heads."

Roberts was pretty tough, too. Once he dropped his shotgun in the canal, stripped down to his skivvies and swam to the bottom in 50 degree water to retrieve it. Another time, Roberts' boat capsized.

"We went down there duck hunting with another friend of ours and Tiny," Laney recalls. "The other guy and Fireball were in one boat and me and Tiny were in another boat. I left the dock 20 seconds before Glenn. He leaves the dock and flips the boat right in the middle of the canal. Tiny says to me, 'Hey, they got a problem back there.' So we turned around and we got back and find Glenn and his friend hanging on to the side of the boat. We just got them over to the dock and got them another boat and we all went on duck hunting."

After leaving the dock, the intrepid hunters would pull off at a marshy area and begin a torturous march through muck and high grass. "We'd walk a quarter of mile," Laney said. "We'd walk through and over all kinds of stuff to get to the ponds where the ducks landed. We'd put out our decoys and get into the foliage and wait for the ducks to show up."

Judge, who went duck hunting just one time with Roberts, said he was a rare triple shot. "He could shoot three ducks with one swing of the barrel. Bam! Bam! Bam! Three ducks would fall."

"Everything we killed, we brought home, never killed just to kill," Laney continued. "Glenn would always rip my ass because he was a better shot than I was. He was much more coordinated. It was always really pretty out there in the morning; still and cold. And the water looked like a mirror. Glenn's dog Rusty was a Chesapeake retriever. That dog would never bring a bird to me. The only person he would give a duck to was Glenn.

"Glenn was an animal person. There are those who can communicate with animals and there are those who can't. I mean any kind of animal, be it a horse or dog, I don't know if it's smell or not."

Later in his life, Fireball added Jolie (French for pretty) to the Roberts' family. She was a black poodle, who liked to snuggle up to her master, a man of wonder and might. "Poodles are people dogs," he told *Sports Illustrated*. "They don't smell and they don't shed. Now, the retriever stays outside. I do mostly duck hunting. We have a real great duck-hunting place right around Cape Kennedy. Of course, I imagine its days are numbered."

He was right. NASA eventually turned Roberts' beloved duck hunting area into a launch pad for the Apollo missions. Maybe that's one reason he never met an astronaut he liked. It seems everything he did, with the exception of slot car racing, came about pretty easily for Roberts; just another reason he was a magnet around people.

"He loved being good at stuff," Judge said. "If he wasn't, he learned it, and then he came back and beat you at it. He would be obsessed with it.

"He was a man's man," she told racing journalist Ken Willis. "Hunted, fished and liked the things most men liked, and was very good at the things he did. Men wanted to be like him, and the women wanted to be with him."

One Dollar Race Cars

In 1956 Fireball Roberts was 27 years old and had conquered all there was to take from the modified ranks. The Grand National Series was in full bloom and the big American automakers were fully involved in stock car racing.

During the 1955-56 racing seasons, Carl Kiekhafer's independently owned Chrysler C-300s were kicking serious ass all over the GN Series, winning everything in sight. Kiekhafer was wealthy, stinking rich. He was the owner of Mercury Outboard Motors and poured large sums of his own money into his racing operation. He used racing as a marketing tool and the high-performance lessons learned at the track were applied to his boat motors. His stunning success, which included back-to-back series championships with Tim Flock and Buck Baker, benefited Chrysler, which saw an unexpected demand for its new C-300 model.

This was all very embarrassing to the folks at General Motors and especially Ford Motor Company, which had no real representation in

NASCAR. Ford tapped 1925 Indianapolis 500 winner Peter DePaolo to start an "independent" Grand National Series race team, which was called DePaolo Engineering. Ford felt it had to do something to curb Chrysler's good fortune in stock car racing.

DePaolo, who started out with Red Vogt running the program, wound up hiring John Holman, who was effective pushing paperwork, ordering supplies, rallying the troops and generally well organized. He was teamed with Ralph Moody, who worked on and raced the cars. They would later own the company, but all these men were on a mission to get Ford's name circulating among racing people.

During this rapid build-up process, Ford went shopping for drivers with racing experience and numbers in their win columns, and landed young Fireball Roberts to a contract through DePaolo Engineering, which was eventually based in Charlotte.

Fireball Roberts competed in 33 of the 56 races staged that season, won five times and finished seventh in points. The following season, it was more of the same. He ran 42 out of 53 races and won eight. In one blazing stretch, from April 7 to April 19, he won three consecutive races. Roberts was now a solid player in the big leagues, with 13 wins, 38 top-five finishes and seven pole positions. There was no going back to the modifieds at this point.

DePaolo sold his operation to Holman and Moody in 1957 who renamed the team Holman-Moody Racing. These were not good times for the racing industry. Another quick history lesson is in order:

Several drivers in various series were killed throughout the 1955 season, including Bill Vukovich, who died in a fiery crash during the Indianapolis 500. Vukovich went to Indy looking for his third consecutive victory in the race.

Later that summer during the 39th running of the 24 Hours of Le Mans sportscar race, driver Pierre Levegh lost control of his Mercedes-Benz racer and crashed into a crowded spectator area, killing more than 100 people. A senator from Oregon tried to seize the moment and called on President Eisenhower to ban all forms of auto racing.

"I think the time has come to forbid automobile racing and similar carnage in the United States," said Sen. Richard Neuberger on the Senate floor.

"His speech," writes historian Greg Fielden, "had the racing fraternity shivering."

The American Automobile Association, which had sanctioned the races at Indianapolis for more than 50 years, said it was going to "disassociate itself from all types of automobile racing in the United States after the 1955 racing season."

Still more bad news in '57 when the Automobile Manufacturers Association – companies like Ford, GM and Chrysler – imposed a racing ban on themselves. All that factory money that had been pouring into the NASCAR ranks was now, officially, cut off.

"There was a truce in 1957 among the manufacturers," Ned Jarrett said. "When Ford pulled out, they sold their drivers' race cars for one dollar each. If you had been driving a race car for Ford, they'd give it to you for one dollar. Fireball made a deal with a guy named Paul Spaulding from Syracuse, New York, with the cars he bought. He didn't drive for long. Junior Johnson started driving for him. That's the car I bought to launch my career into Grand National racing, in the latter part of 1959, because Spaulding was building a new Dodge for Junior for Darlington. So, I bought that car – with a bad check. That's the car Fireball had been driving in '57."

Drivers were scrambling for deals. Some of the biggest names in stock car racing vanished overnight and NASCAR needed a bolt of lightning to draw fan support. As Fielden writes in his *Forty Years of Stock Car Racing* series: "NASCAR badly needed a new star to replace the dozens who had vanished – a fresh face who could draw admiration from the fans and take the sport to a higher plateau. A single creator, it has been said, gives a show its characteristic look, sound and momentum. Edward Glenn 'Fireball' Roberts, Jr. was NASCAR's savior in 1958."

Roberts wound up with car owner Frank Strickland, from Atlanta, in 1958 and became something of a sensation. He made only 10 starts during the 51-race campaign, eight with Strickland, and won six races, including the prestigious Southern 500 and two other superspeedway events. He finished 11th in points, despite skipping 80 percent of the schedule, and led nearly half the laps he turned during the season. Somebody, other than racers, was watching, because Roberts was bestowed the Florida Sports Writers Professional Athlete of the Year Award in 1958.

Writes Fielden: "It was the first time the coveted award went to a race car driver. The trophy he received would be one of Roberts' most prized possessions until the day he died. He felt the award helped stock car racing finally make the mark in the sporting world."

Roberts had caught the big wave and planned to ride that baby all the way to shore. He had become a star when drivers were beginning to come into their own as personalities and celebrities. Race fans started to take notice of the driver behind the machine, not just the make of the car they were driving.

Chris Economaki, who did some work as a track announcer, remembers the transition. "I started announcing in NASCAR in 1951 at the beach, and when the Daytona speedway opened," he said. "In the mid-1950s, I used to be the announcer at Darlington, and the emphasis up to that point was on the car. It was Ford vs. Chevy vs. Dodge. Then all of a sudden, the emphasis changed from the machine, to the man and we talked more about the driver and the personality of the people manning the machines than we did the car. It was a distinctive and organized change."

The man benefiting the most from this change of race fan perception was Roberts, who had the catchy nickname, heavy right foot, rugged good looks and spoke words the average person could understand. His career was about to rocket to new levels, where he would take his place alongside the most famous athletes of that era. He would be described as the "Mickey Mantle of stock car racing" – or the biggest star in his sport.

Stock car racing was at the doorstep of a new age, a golden age, and Fireball Roberts would be right there to show everybody around.

1960
9 Starts, 6 Poles
9 Races Led
1,338 Laps, 578 Laps Led
2 Wins, Rank: 29
Winnings: $19,895

One Night at the Martinique...

Judy Judge describes her childhood in Florida as idyllic. She was born to William and Dorothy Judge, who raised their two daughters in a big house overlooking the Halifax River, which split the area in two. There was the peninsula side (a sandy barrier island) and the mainland. Judy's sister, Patty, arrived three years later. The house was in Holly Hill, which is a small municipality on the mainland side nestled between Daytona Beach, to the south, and Ormond Beach, to the north.

These days there's a house on every lot along the river in Holly Hill, but back then, in the 1940s, the town had a much more rural feel. The Judge family kept horses on their property and riding was one of Judy's favorite pastimes.

The Judge house became known in the neighborhood as an animal sanctuary. "Because of the horses, anybody that had lost or found an animal, or had an animal they didn't want, brought them to our house because we had them all over the place," Judy says. "We all took care of them, found a home for them and kept some."

Dorothy was the typical stay-at-home mother who doted over her two daughters, leaving those really tough punishments in the hands of her husband. "Just wait until your father comes home!" Dorothy would let her husband hand down punishments when their daughters got into trouble.

William (his friends called him Billy) was an attorney, and during his career he served as a state attorney and municipal judge, which prompted a laugh from Judy. He was named after *both* his grandfathers, who were each William. When he earned an appointment to the local court, his full title and name was: Judge William William Judge.

He moved here with his family from Pennsylvania when he was 13 years old. Judy's mother was born and raised in the area. Dorothy's kin had settled in the region generations before giving them the distinction as an "old Daytona family."

As children, Judy and Patty had plenty of adult supervision because Dorothy's parents lived in the breeze-swept house for a time while a house of theirs was being built, only blocks from the Judge residence.

"They were always in and out," Judy says. "We saw our grandparents a lot as children. There was plenty of room. It was a lot of property, I mean, a lot of property. It seemed bigger when I was a child but the house is still there and it's still huge. It's in disrepair now. My friends who have gone by there tell me, 'Oh, it looks so bad.' But when I was growing up, it was a beautiful house.

"Our house was a big, two-story house," she continued. "When my parents bought it, it was a hundred years old. It was just beautiful.

We had our horses in the backyard and we could ride all day and that's what Patty and I did."

The Judge family wasn't rich, but they were comfortable and there was no question that Judge Judge was in charge of the household. Pragmatic and stern, he had a say in everything that happened within the family unit.

"Tough guy? Yes, he was of that era but he loved us and made sure we had everything we wanted," Judy said. "He was a hands-off father, work all day, come home at night. Mother was there for us every day and did everything for us. Daddy was always proud of us but he never took us out; he didn't go to any football or basketball games when I was cheerleading or anything like that. He didn't do that kind of thing. He was an authority figure, not only to me, but to everybody, like my friends. You didn't want to do anything to upset him and we didn't. I guess you could say we led fairly sheltered lives."

When Judy reached high school, she avoided trouble, made good grades and stayed in cheerleading for four years. "There were six of us girls (cheerleaders) and we hung around together and have remained friends. We still see each other from time to time. My mother always wanted everybody, my friends, at our house, so everybody was at our house and that was nice."

At 17, Judy graduated from the old Mainland High School in 1955, but the joy of finishing her secondary education was diminished by the death of her mother on July 2 (make note of that date) of that year. "She had a very long, awful battle with cancer," she said.

As Dorothy withered away from the disease, William turned to the bottle for solace, and became a hard drinker for several years. The very foundation of Judy's dream childhood was coming apart at the seams.

"I went to the University of Florida in the fall of 1955 and stayed until Christmastime," Judy said. "My father had already remarried. My stepmother and my sister were having a terrible time, so I dropped out and came home to take care of Patty. Daddy sold our house and we moved over to the beachside, a street named Oleander. That house had an apartment in the back and that's where Patty and I lived. I worked at the telephone company for a few years, then begged daddy to go back to college. I mean I had to beg him. I went to Stetson in DeLand because it was the closest college to Daytona. I commuted between Daytona and DeLand the first year because Patty was still in high school and needed me. And that's when I met Glenn."

She met Glenn for the first time at the Martinique, which was a lively little nightclub designed for college-aged kids.

"Everybody went there because they always had a great band," Judy said. "You could get in the door if you were 18 and dance. You could drink if you were 21. So we all went in there as a group, all the time, to dance. Glenn said I danced with him one night when we first started going there, and I didn't remember it."

The next time they danced, which was late in 1958, they hit it off. "We just started talking and he was adorable," she swooned. "That's when he told me his name was Bobby Edwards. I had never been to a race. We didn't go to races because 'nice girls' didn't do that. I didn't know who he was, but I met him at the Martinique, we danced and had a good time. I met him there for several months. I would go in there just to see if he was there. He finally asked me out and took me to Orlando to meet friends of his, Dick Joslin and his wife."

Joslin was a short track racer that Roberts knew from the racing circuit, and was part of the young driver's inner circle of friends. When Roberts showed up in Orlando with Judy, Joslin played along with the Bobby Edwards story.

"Yeah, he (Joslin) did that," Judy says, rolling her eyes. "We started dating after that. He would come to the house to get me, the apartment in the back. I had no idea who he was, had no idea, but I liked him a lot. He was not interested in any kind of permanent relationship; *he just was not interested*. But he was very interested when he was with me. That went on until the big speedway in Daytona opened."

And that's when Judy Judge discovered the true identity of Bobby Edwards.

"A friend came down from North Carolina and asked me to go to the race with him, and I said I didn't want to go, and he said, 'Oh, yeah you do. It will be a lot of fun.' And we went, and it was the race on Saturday, the day before the first Daytona 500. My friend says he was rooting for Joe Weatherly and asked me who I was cheering for. I told him, 'I have no idea, I don't know anybody, buy a program and I'll pick somebody.'

"My friend bought a program and I started to look at the driver pictures and there was Glenn's face. I told my friend, 'I know that guy.' And he didn't believe me. 'Oh yeah, I know him.' I could not believe that's who it was; I just could not believe it – Fireball Roberts, for god's sake. I told my friend I knew him and that's who I'd root for and he said, 'You'll have to prove that to me.'"

Daytona International Speedway had just opened and it was easy to get from place to place. Only the garage area was off limits to race fans and spectators. There wasn't a myriad of gates and fences like today's maze. "It was big, but not so fancy," Judy said. "So we walked down to this chained fence, and by the concession stand. I saw somebody walking by in the inside, and said, 'Tell Fireball Roberts to come over here.' And this guy in the garage says, 'Yeah right.' And I said, 'No, tell him to come over here right now.' So the man walks over to this guy sitting over on the pit wall, tapped him on the shoulder and it was Glenn. He got up and walked over. 'Well, hello Fireball!' "

They met back at the club that night and Roberts was able to smooth things over explaining that he knew race car drivers were taboo for 'nice girls.' He didn't want to scare her off because of his profession. The Bobby Edwards ploy worked because Judy never looked at Roberts like he was the stereotypical, good-for-nothing, low-life, stock car driver. "He just wasn't ever that to me," she said softly. "He was never Fireball Roberts to me. He was Glenn.

"Patty had gone with me to the Martinique with me that night, and we drove him to his car. He asked me if I was going to the race the next day, I said, 'What race?' He said, 'Judy, the big race is tomorrow.' I didn't know there was another race. I said, 'No!' He said he'd call me, and he did. And I was never with anybody else after that."

Yes, sweet and innocent Judy Judge was head over heels in love with a race car driver who was gaining national fame with each passing season. At this time in his life, he was heading into the prime of his career, and stirring up gossip all over town. When he was in town and not racing, Judy, the college student, was on Glenn Roberts' arm, out under the city lights. With her trouble at home – her daddy drinking and his new wife alienating Judy and Patty – Roberts was like manna from heaven. Little did she know there was yet another bigger surprise to spring out of the box.

By this time Roberts was driving a car owned and prepared by Smokey Yunick, the famed racing mechanic with a truck shop and racing garage over on Beach Street – the Best Damn Garage in Town – not far from where Roberts used to work at Fish Carburetors. Roberts and Yunick teamed up in a Pontiac sponsored by local car dealer Jim Stephens. After winning the inaugural Firecracker 250, Roberts and Yunick made an appearance at Stephens Pontiac with the race-winning car and drew a large crowd.

Daytona Beach and surrounding community was a small town.

It wasn't New York City. There were only so many places to go eat dinner or drink. People knew people who knew people and when Roberts won the 1959 race, the news that the driver was seeing a beautiful young college girl finally reached Doris Roberts, Glenn's wife of nine years. Doris thought she could take care of this whole situation with one phone call to Judge William William Judge, who stormed into Stephen's Pontiac and confronted the famed Fireball.

The next day Judy got the ultimatum from her father – either stop seeing Roberts or you are no longer part of the family. "I chose Glenn," Judy said, "because at that point, there was no family." She never thought she would ever find herself in this situation, as the girlfriend of a married man, who was a damned race car driver of all things.

"It was worse than horrible," she said. "It was the worst thing I could think of and the worst thing with my family, too. It was awful, just awful, and it just didn't get better. Glenn knew, *he knew*, what it was costing me, and that was hard for him, and he became a lot more attentive."

Still, she was a mental mess after deciding to buck her family and begin this journey with Roberts. "I can't tell you, I just can't tell you what it was like. Glenn was the lifeboat and yet he was also the anchor. He told me this sad story about his marriage and what it was. I believed him, because what choice did I have? I knew there had to be something wrong, because he was with me four nights a week.

"He was a player, he had dated everybody, he was well known as a race car driver. But I wasn't in the same circle, I didn't know any of that! I think that's what really attracted him to me, that I was innocent, I was in college, I was a virgin. He was making a list and checking it twice. When all this happened, well, it got out of hand with him, too. All of a sudden, he was in over his head." When their relationship become serious, friends say Roberts made a dramatic lifestyle change, remaining faithful to Judge.

After refusing to leave Roberts, Judy moved out of the Judge house and rented an apartment. Roberts set up camp there, too, spending four or five nights a week with Judy, who continued her education at Stetson. On some race weekends, she would fly up to meet him. During the summer, when she wasn't in school, she was a regular on the Grand National Series circuit. When they were

in town, Roberts would appease his wife by taking her out to dinner almost every Saturday night. "What a lovely thing," Judy says today. "He'd take Doris out to dinner, then about 11 o'clock, he'd be at the apartment."

Doris would telephone Judy and tell her about all the other women he had bedded during their marriage. Sometimes, she would show up at the apartment. "None of it was very pleasant," Judy says. "If she knew Glenn was out of town, she would go to a pay phone and call the apartment. When I answered the phone, she would say something awful and leave the phone off the hook. That would busy my phone line until somebody came along and hung up the phone where she had called from. My phone would be useless for one, sometimes two days."

As the harassment escalated, Glenn took Judy to a local gun shop and bought her a Dieringer 25, a petite pocket handgun. It didn't have the firepower to stop a big man, but it was stout enough to bring down the fury of an angry wife. "He told me to shoot *anyone* who came in the apartment," Judy said. "He took me out to the woods and taught me how to shoot it."

Judy said there was one time when she and Doris had one almost civil conversation. "Yeah, I guess we did, and she told me I was one of a list of many women, and that he would leave me and come back to her. He always did. She told me all kinds of things that were not nice and not true. I don't think she ever knew him very well; she surely didn't know the same man I knew. But they had Pam, and Pam was a real hard thing for Glenn to deal with. She was his child and he didn't want to do anything to hurt her, and he didn't want to do anything publicity-wise that would be bad. He tried and tried and tried for two years to get her to get a divorce."

In those days, family law was tilted well in favor of women. Glenn could not get a divorce without consent from Doris. "It was different then, very different," Judy said. "He really was concerned about the publicity. He didn't want bad publicity or the publicity that we were together, even though everybody knew it. We did it his way."

In very short order, the racing community got to meet Miss Judy Judge, who became a regular on the tour. Competitors, track owners and the media looked the other way when she became a regular. "That's just the way it was in those days," Humpy Wheeler says. "Media intensity not being what is today, people didn't say anything about it. I think it was the culture of NASCAR in those days. There was a different moral standard, but one of the things you didn't do, you didn't judge other people. That just wasn't done by most of the people. It was live and let live."

Said Ned Jarrett: "We all knew about Judy and we really didn't give a second thought."

A Pair of Aces

Why the hell didn't somebody think of this sooner? Over there on Beach Street, at the Best Damn Garage in Town, you have got Smokey Yunick, who was one of the premier racing mechanics of the era, and not more than two miles away was Glenn "Fireball" Roberts, who could run the wheels off a stock car and was becoming one of the biggest stars in the sport.

Two men, great at what they did in racing, and yet they ran on the same tracks but in their own orbits. Funny isn't it, that one small town in Florida was overflowing with so much racing talent? Roberts had already worked with three of NASCAR's greatest mechanics in Marshall Teague, Ray Fox and Red Vogt. And now he was about to become part of one of the greatest mechanic-driver tag-teams in the history of racing.

Yunick was a workaholic racing genius. Roberts was young, confident and chock plum full of racing savvy. They would combine to become an unstoppable force especially at NASCAR's enormous new speed palaces. And, wouldn't you know, the biggest and fastest track of them all was being built in their neighborhood by NASCAR boss man Bill France Sr.

It seems all the powers of the stock car racing universe were converging on Daytona Beach to make something special, very special, happen. And it did, but only after Roberts suffered the loss of his first racing mentor.

France built Daytona International Speedway because developers were closing in on his famed Beach & Road Course. He didn't own any of that land, just leased it in the winter to stage his races. As his son, William C. France says, "We charged people to stand on somebody else's property." He knew the beach course days were numbered and used all his resources, called in all his favors to build the $3 million, 2.5-mile, "D" shaped, high-banked superspeedway on swampland west of town.

Yunick takes credit for "running" the first race car at the track. Well, sort of. He was heading up to the 1958 Indianapolis 500 towing his race car behind him when he detoured off Highway 92 (now International Speedway Boulevard) and did a quick lap around the course, which had not been paved.

After the track was paved and the asphalt had cured, Marshall Teague asked to run speed laps in the Sumar Special, an Indy-car

See the black and gold Pontiac?

That's it, number 22.

There, sir, is a racer.

If you're sitting in the grandstand, notice how many heads turn when that one buzzes by.

If you're in the infield near the pits, perhaps you've already noticed that more than one mechanic whips out his stop watch when she starts cutting hot laps.

But you can't fully appreciate her until you see her from behind. There, friend, is the most looked-at rear end in stock car racing, including those that were wrapped up in bathing suits at Daytona Beach last month.

You can guess who does the looking—the guys who drive the other cars. I don't mean to say that they enjoy it, however. Fact is, some see a whole lot less of number 22's rear end than others. And sometimes I think a few of those fellows are out there just to see if they can show number 22 the rear end of their machine, if only for one lap.

I don't suppose I have to tell you that none of these racers run by remote control. There is a man behind the steering wheel of every one of them. Like the cars, some are better than others. Some are great. Believe me, the driver in black and gold Pontiac number 22 is a great one.

They call him Fireball Roberts. His name is really Glenn Roberts, but one spring morning about 18 years ago some kids were playing baseball on a sandlot diamond in Florida and they needed a pitcher. A big Greek boy was catching when Glenn Roberts sent his high, hard one sailing toward the plate. "Hey!" whistled the catcher, "you're a real fireball." It's been Fireball ever since.

Last month at Daytona Beach, Fireball drove number 22 faster than anyone had ever driven for 500 consecutive miles. He averaged better than 152 miles per hour in winning the Daytona 500. They saw a lot of number 22's rear end that day.

It was a sweet one for Fireball in more ways than one. Last October in Charlotte, N. C., he was running in his favorite position—out front—when a tire exploded, hurling number 22 violently against the guard rail. The crippled automobile slithered down the track almost to a stop when another race car smashed into it at better than 100. Roberts called it the closest call of his life. "If I'd been hit on the driver's side that would have been it," he remarked as two ambulance drivers picked bits of glass out of his eyes.

Then a few people began to suggest that maybe Fireball Roberts wouldn't be going quite so hard next time out. Maybe, they guessed, Fireball had more than the wind knocked out of him.

But they were wrong. "The next one" was Daytona and at Daytona he was unbeatable. He ran a 25-mile race, a 100-mile race and a 500-mile race during Speed Weeks and won them all.

Perhaps his critics did him a favor. Perhaps they have launched him on the biggest season of his career, bigger even than 1958 when he teamed with an Atlanta mechanic named Paul McDuffie and won two 500-milers and four 250-milers.

Perhaps his destiny is stock car racing's first grand slam—sweeping all four classics in a single year: the Daytona 500 at Daytona, the Atlanta 500 in Atlanta, the World 600 at Charlotte, N. C., and the Southern 500 at Darlington, South Carolina.

He led them all last year. Who is to say that he could not win them all this year?

At any rate, he has won at Daytona and now he wants to win in Atlanta. Then Charlotte. Then Darlington.

His guileless strategy is a fresh breeze in this day of bluff and counterbluff—get out front and stay there.

When they drop the green flag on the Atlanta 500, watch black and gold Pontiac number 22. You'll see what I mean.

—Max Muhleman

Max Muhleman

owned by Chapman Root. During the closed-course speed run on Feb. 11, 1959, Teague's machine bottomed out in the tri-oval, went into a tumble and killed the veteran driver, who had made two Indy 500 starts and won several NASCAR races.

It was an omen of sorts of things to come at the big track. Thirty six people have died at Daytona, including a spectator and most recently a track worker. Dale Earnhardt succumbed there in 2001 on the last lap of the Daytona 500. No matter. Competitors come by the droves each year because Daytona is like a religious temple of racing during its Speedweeks program, three weeks of tire squealing, fender-bending pleasure. Rev. Hal Marchman calls Speedweeks "Redneck High Holy Days" and the Daytona 500 is the Holy Grail. Only the weeks leading up to the Indianapolis 500 generate as much excitement and electricity around a racetrack.

The Indy 500 goes back to 1911 when Ray Harroun won the inaugural. While Daytona didn't have a speedway until 1959, the area's racing history goes back to 1903 when those two brave souls saddled up on their horseless carriages to do battle on the beach. That is why a Daytona victory carries more value than the next track on the schedule. It comes backed with more than 100 years of racing tradition.

Yunick was racing with driver Paul Goldsmith during the late 1950s. "Goldy" was versatile because he could run the stocks and wasn't afraid to buckle into an Indy-style car. They teamed up to win the last Grand National Series on the beach, but parted company after that '58 victory. Yunick was becoming more and more intrigued with racing at Indianapolis because the rule book was so skinny. But he had a backdoor deal with Pontiac for 1959.

In his autobiography, Yunick says Roberts initiated the contact to drive the car, which would carry the Stephen's Pontiac colors into battle: "When Fireball Roberts hears Paul is gone to [Ray] Nichels, he comes by and asks to drive a '59 Pontiac I'm building for [Bunkie] Knudsen [from GM]. Well even though we are kinda neighbors, and

I consider him one of the four NASCAR driving aces, I'm hesitant to hook up with him. I have a total of one paid helper and a couple of goofy volunteers (and I say that reverently, without 'em I could not of done one-third of what I did). I also know Fireball has two allergies, asthma and work, and he don't like to tow the racecar. I don't enjoy towing either."

By this time in Roberts' career, he had grown weary of the road and complexities of a small racing operation. After all, he had barnstormed the country as a modified racer for six years, then had run 85 Grand National races from 1956-58. He wanted to compete on a limited schedule and concentrate on NASCAR's biggest racing events, the ones that offered the biggest prize money and most exposure. He had

more on his mind than racing; he had many other interests, and of course, including that wife-girlfriend thing going on.

Yunick continues: "Fireball had the skill and the balls, and he was the smartest of the drivers. I think he was the first full-time race driver. Everyone else had a 'day job.' He rated all his competitors, noted their shortcomings, considered all other race cars as to speed and durability and spent a lot of time developing pit strategy. He didn't care too much for my method of running a maximum or minimum lap time, don't get lapped, and start racing last one hundred miles. His plan was simple: Sit on the pole, and lead every lap.

"I did decide to race with Fireball. We raced together damn near four years with Pontiacs, '59, '60, '61 and part of '62. If Fireball would have had a tire that could have stood up under the punishment he put on them, his record would be something that would have never been equaled."

Tires were a major problem for NASCAR drivers. Before a true racing tire was developed by Firestone and Goodyear, tires were always a wild card at asphalt tracks. Fireball's friend Max Muhleman explained the difficulty racing on this crude rubber.

"From 1958 to the early 1960s was a tire blowing era," Muhleman said. "When a tire would blow back then it would sound like a cannon firing in the harbor to repel the pirates. They were huge explosions. You don't hear it when they cut a tire now, you don't hear it when they hit the wall. Every head would turn toward these blowouts because the sound was so powerful. They sounded like big guns in battle. When they would blow, the car had a mind of its own and it tried to leap out of the racetrack. It took quite a ballsy guy to sit in a car and know his chances are one out of six that something is going to blow out, and the faster he would go, the worse it was going to be. Fireball got a real kick out of a song that came out during that time called *'Hello Walls.'*"

The song, by Country and Western legend Faron Young, had absolutely nothing to do with racing, but saying hello to walls around the racing circuit was commonplace for Roberts, who always pushed his equipment past its ability. (Roberts' favorite song, his theme song, was *'Ahab the Arab, Sheik of the Burnin' Sand'* performed by Ray Stevens. Said Spiers: "I guess that wouldn't be too politically correct today.")

In a story he penned for *Circle Track*, Yunick writes:

> Fireball was forever saying hello to walls, banging into walls, trading paint with walls, and otherwise becoming intimate with them…Not that Fireball was personally at fault. At that time we were entering an era of stock car racing when we had way too much race car and not enough tire. We had superspeedways, and we had speed averages faster than those at Indianapolis,

but we didn't yet have adequate rubber. What was worse still, the tires didn't yet have safety inner-liners. So, whenever a tire blew, you went out of control and nailed the wall.

The faster you raced, the sooner you busted a tire, and that meant Fireball busted the most, because he was the quickest of them all. 'Run 'er flat out, belly to the ground' – that's the way we talked. Fireball started all that. He was the original hero of the superspeedways.

It was a nerve-racking time for me, having to stand there in the pits watching and waiting for him to blow another one. But it was worse for him, naturally, because his butt was the one strapped in the car. He used to set himself up to try to work the groove up by the wall, so that when a tire did let go, he wouldn't have such a running start at the wall.

Yunick said Roberts would always fight the wheel after the right front tire blew out and the car smacked the wall. He would take his foot off the brake to try to save the car and inevitably, the car would loop and hit the wall on the left side of the car, doubling the repair time for Yunick. Yunick made this suggestion to Roberts. He said, "Next time you bust a tire, how about keeping the brakes locked up and seeing what happens? Quit trying to save the son of a bitch. Maybe we can save ourselves some of these both-side repair numbers.

We're slap out of wall jobs."

Roberts tried it at Charlotte Motor Speedway in 1961 and just about got killed in that accident with Bill Morgan. "That Pontiac just went to crap," Yunick wrote for *Circle Track*. "It threw parts everywhere. It heaved its front end assembly more than half a mile until it finally landed in a field across the street from the track. 'Not a very good idea of mine, was it?' " I asked Fireball afterward. 'I just wish you'd been inside it with me,' he answered.

Daytona International Speedway was like a giant beast compared to some of the teeny little dirt tracks that dominated the Grand National Series in 1959. It was 2.5 miles of asphalt and had 31-degree banking. Zora Duntov, a General Motors design engineer, and Yunick were gazing at this titan when it first opened with local sports editor Bernard Kahn in the vicinity. "Driving it is something like playing a violin with one string," Duntov said of Daytona. Without hesitation, Yunick replied, "Yes, and the driver better be a virtuoso."

The first Daytona 500 was staged nine days after Teague's death. Roberts, driving the No. 3 Stephen's Pontiac prepped by Yunick, started 46th and finished 45th in a rather inauspicious beginning to what would become a tremendous union. Maybe Roberts had other things on his mind that day; it was the day after he confessed to Judy Judge his true identity.

Fireball and Smokey returned to their home track with a vengeance for the Fourth of July Firecracker 250. Roberts sat on the pole position and captured the race at an average speed of 140.581 mph in the

No. 3 Pontiac. And the day after that, Roberts had the parking lot confrontation with one angry Judge Judge, who more or less disowned his daughter for dating the popular and married race car driver.

Roberts and Yunick raced five times, three starts at Daytona, in '59 and came away with that summer victory. Roberts made three other starts with three other car owners that season. His best finish was sixth in a Buck Baker-owned Chevy at Atlanta.

The real magic happened when Fireball was behind the wheel of the Smokey-built Pontiac. In 1960, running his signature No. 22,

they raced nine times and won twice, a 100-mile qualifying race at Daytona and the first race at Atlanta International Raceway. In '61 Roberts had six poles and two victories and was about 25 miles away from winning the Daytona 500 before he had engine problems. Roberts and Yunick shared the same passion for the sport. Said Yunick's friend Bob Snodgrass: "They had the overwhelming desire to win at almost any cost."

"There were always premier driver-crew chief combinations, but none of them got any publicity," Chris Economaki said. "That was the first combination that got some. You really have to remember that Smokey Yunick was a tremendously intelligent man. He was an exceptional talent; he really was. In my mind he was the first of the leading crew chiefs. He understood that the car made the difference. He was the first guy to understand it. Up until Smokey's time, everyone figured the driver made the difference."

Leonard Wood, from the famed Wood Brothers Racing team, said Smokey and Fireball were damn near invincible when they joined forces. "Smokey had a great car and when you got a great car and great driver it's going to go off good and that's where you get your recognition," Wood said.

Opposing mechanics and drivers went to NASCAR and accused Smokey and Fireball of cheating, which always brought a wide smile to the face of NASCAR technical director Norris Friel. "Hah," he'd say, "they fuss about Fireball but I can tell you his secret. When those other guys are letting off (the gas), he's still going deeper into the corners."

"Fireball had a real good mechanical knowledge," Humpy Wheeler said. "He could tell you what was going on underneath that race car at a time when a lot of drivers couldn't because, again the superspeedway era was just coming in. I think the ultimate compliment was paid to Fireball when Smokey asked him to be his driver. Smokey's probably the toughest guy on drivers that ever lived. Smokey wouldn't put up with anything; not with a race driver. At that time, Smokey was getting more horsepower, considerable more horsepower than anybody else on the track."

Then there was 1962, which yielded one of the greatest racing seasons ever imagined for a driver. And it was a time when Roberts began to sort out his personal life and found direction. He was beginning to formulate a plan for his future.

"He wanted to be more," Judy Judge said. "He thought of himself as a professional athlete and he thought he could be more than a race driver. That was his goal."

1961

22 Starts, 6 Poles
13 Races Led
5,075 Laps, 1,002 Laps Led
2 Wins, Rank: 5
Winnings: $50,267

Congratulations Fireball!

In the winter of 1961-62, Smokey Yunick worked meticulously on the No. 22 Pontiac that he would ship across town to Daytona International Speedway for the '62 Speedweeks program. Yunick had won the 1961 Daytona 500 with another Daytona Beach driver, Marvin Panch, at the wheel of his No. 20 Pontiac, only after Roberts' car suffered a mechanical problem in the closing laps of NASCAR's biggest and richest race. Panch wisely took his share of the winnings and bought property out in the sticks west of Daytona and built "Pancho's Rancho," a house and racing garage complex.

As the racers gathered for the 1962 Speedweeks program, all eyes were on Smokey and Fireball and their black Pontiac with gold trim. Up to that point, Roberts had won the '59 summer race and qualifying races in '60 and '61. He also sat on the pole position – the fastest car in qualifying – for both big Daytona races in '61. They were the hottest driver-mechanic combo on the circuit. Max Muhleman remembers the enchantment of the No. 22.

"I thought Smokey had sort of a charisma all his own, too," Muhleman said. "To me he was as interesting a guy as any of the drivers. I would later come to feel he definitely was. Fireball was fast and driving the best-looking car out there and he had a great name. It was a Hollywood type name. And he backed it up with a quiet dignity."

"He won the Daytona 500 in 1962, but he was already Fireball before then. The fact of the matter is he probably led more races than anybody. In the races he entered/led, he probably had an extraordinary statistical edge; not in races finished and won. This guy would go right to the front and he was very frequently the pole winner and that was even more of macho thing than it is today. It was just 'Fireball fast,' you know. Here's this guy from Florida, his friend and car builder, and these guys are the best driver and mechanic combination going. People wanted to see him. I give a lot of charismatic credit to his nickname because he backed it up. His nickname wasn't Slim or Bubba or Lefty that we think of as common male nicknames. It was Fireball for crying out loud. He ran like a Fireball; it was self perpetuating.

"Fireball's legacy was written on the backs of Smokey Yunick's black and gold No. 22 cars. If you went to a race, you went to see Fireball," he added.

And they got an eyeful in Daytona in '62. What a show of brute horsepower and driving finesse. First, Roberts captured the coveted pole position then won a 40-lap (100 mile) qualifying race, leading the field around the 2.5-mile course for 33 of those laps. In the Daytona 500, he started at the top of the field but his all-out driving style nearly cost him the race. Roberts ran out of fuel twice in the early part of the race and had to work his way back to the front, leading 144 of 200 laps to score the victory. In the closing laps, he had 24-year-old Richard Petty, the future star of the series, hanging on his rear bumper. It was one of the most dominating performances by a driver in all the history of racing and elevated Roberts to the very top of the competitor pyramid.

A funny thing happened after that big victory. After Roberts had made all the required rounds to speak to the media and meet various racing big shots and honchos, the track was practically void of people and it was almost dark.

"The Goodyear blimp came over the speedway and I was leaning against the hood of our car, and looked up and on the side of the blimp, in lights, it said, 'Congratulations Fireball!' We had a little moment there," Judge said. "He went to change clothes and I had his wallet, watch and inhaler and I handed it all to him. He asks me, 'Where are the car keys?' And I told him, 'I don't know. You didn't give them to me.' He looked through the car window and there the keys were in the ignition. He was so pissed. He was furious. He was walking around the car trying to figure out how to get into it. There was nobody there. He finally decided he had to break a window to get into the car. He picked up a rock and was getting ready to hit the window, when a policeman rolled up and started giving him some mouth about stealing the car.

He said 'No, no, I locked my keys in it. I just won the race and I got to get out of here.' He showed him his driver's license, so the policeman opened the door for him – after Glenn signed an autograph for him."

Roberts made good use of his fame. He bought an airplane in 1961 and used it not only to go from race to race but to make personal appearances throughout the country. As he piled up wins in NASCAR's big races, the demand for his services escalated. Judge, who taught at Holly Hill Elementary School during the 1961-62 school year, quit her job and stayed on the road with Roberts, who taught her how to fly. No need to call the FAA because she didn't have a license.

"When he bought the airplane, I was never afraid to fly with him," she said. "He made me learn how to fly, so if he had a heart attack or something, I could get us down safely. No license, but I flew, took off and landed. He was proud of that."

Judge told Deb Williams from *Winston Cup Scene* about the time they took a sightseeing flyover of Washington, D.C. "I had never seen Washington before," she said. "My job was to navigate. So we're flying over Washington, and he's pointing out this and he's pointing out that and he's telling me things, and all of a sudden I look up and, on either wingtip, are jet fighter pilots. They've got their flaps down, their gear down, everything is down to keep them in the air going as slow as we're going. They tell us to land immediately. 'Andrews Air Force Base, land.' They met us when we touched down with jeeps, with rifles pulled. We stopped that airplane and they pulled my bag out first. I went in one jeep. Glenn got out and went in another jeep. I was so scared. We had flown right over the White House. He's telling them he's real sorry, and

I'm telling them that I don't know what they're talking about. The FBI came. It was bad! It was scary! I don't know how many hours later they let us go."

Speaking of Judy Judge, things were going much better on the home front. Roberts had finally talked Doris into filing for divorce and he started stashing all his extra money away in a safety deposit box in order to reach a one-time, marriage-ending settlement. He wanted the lawful union over, once and for all. He didn't want to owe Doris a penny when the paperwork finally snaked its way out of the courthouse.

"If he couldn't count on you, you were not going to be around, period," Judge said. "When he cut somebody out, he cut them out of his life. He didn't want anything to do with Doris (after the divorce). That's why that divorce was so explicit. He knew he'd have to make a big payout and he didn't want to have to keep paying Doris."

A strange thing occurred soon after Roberts' Daytona 500 victory. Yunick thought Roberts had lost his driving edge, lost his nerve and wasn't comfortable in a race car any longer. Yunick explained his theory in his *Circle Track* piece:

> Fireball surely was the best stock car driver of his time. But nobody's perfect. Nobody lasts forever. Age, loss of will, the survival instinct, all those things slowly destroy the race driver. And the racing mechanic, too, for that matter.
>
> By 1962, Fireball was all through. And he probably had put on 10 to 15 pounds that he hadn't had before.
>
> "Something the matter with the car's seat?" I asked him not long after we'd won the Daytona 500. "You want to change it?"
>
> "No," he said. "Why?"
>
> "Well," I said, "you just don't look comfortable in

the car anymore."

And he didn't. The last season we ran together, I started seeing the seat gap getting him. What I call "the seat gap" occurs when, instead of relaxing and leaning back into the seat, a driver begins hunching anxiously over the steering wheel, opening a gap between himself

and the back of the seat. Fireball was jittery. All that wallbanging finally had taken its toll...

..."Fireball," I finally said to him, "you've got a problem. And I've got a problem. I've never had a guy hurt or killed and I'm not starting now. In my opinion, you've had it, and I'm not going to race with you anymore."

He got mad as hell.

"Now," I said, "before you make a big deal out of this, or go tell the newspapers you've been fired, it's not that way. I've already talked to Banjo Matthews. I'm giving all the Pontiacs to him and he still wants you to race them. I'm also giving all the engines to Banjo and I'll help him any way I can. Personally, I think it'd be better if you quit, but I don't expect you to."

And that was the end of it.

Or it was, anyway, until July when he and Banjo came down for the Firecracker 250 and got into some trouble. I helped them get their engine straightened out, but I doubt I was even in the pits when they won the race. Afterward, Fireball and I didn't speak. He quite obviously had disliked what I'd told him.

Judge disagrees that Roberts lost his racing nerve after the '62 Daytona 500 but said during that season he began plotting an exit strategy; to leave race car driving behind and begin work in public relations and maybe do some television and radio racing commentary. The electronic media was beginning to show some interest in racing at that point.

Roberts may not have had Yunick for a crew chief, but he still had the Yunick-branded equipment, which had been delivered to Matthews. In their first race together at North Wilkesboro (North Carolina) Speedway, Roberts finished fourth. When they returned to Daytona International Speedway in the summer, Roberts took the Firecracker 250 becoming the first driver to sweep both Grand National events at the big track.

The 1962 season was playing out like a Hollywood script.

"We had a good time that year," Judge said. "That was a good year. That was also the year he decided he was quitting, as soon as the divorce was final. He wanted enough money so we didn't have to work and he wanted opportunities to work."

Again, Roberts broke the mold of stock car drivers of the era and accepted an entry in the 24 Hours of Le Mans to drive an exotic Ferrari owned by Luigi Chinetti. Roberts had driven a Chinetti Ferrari in a three-hour sportscar race at Daytona (just seven days before the Daytona 500), impressing all in the wine-and-cheese racing crowd with an sixth-place finish, second in class. *Automobile Quarterly* wrote: "Fireball drove a tremendous race, finishing second in class to Stirling Moss. Since Moss' Berlinetta sported a full Testa Rossa engine against Roberts "stock" Ferrari powerplant, this feat was all the more impressive." Longtime road racer Bob Snodgrass said some of the high-brow racers snickered after seeing Roberts' driving suit. "He had sewn a powder puff on his sleeve to wipe his goggles," Snodgrass said. "Sir Stirling Moss gave Fireball a pretty hard time about it, but after the race Stirling said, 'He may have a lady's powder puff sewn on his suit, but he's awfully fast." Moss was one of the top international drivers of the day.

Bill France Sr. and his teen-age son Jim made the trip to watch the spectacle in France and cheer on Roberts, the hometown driving hero. Roberts was paired with Bob Grossman in the North American Racing Team Ferrari 250 GT, very much like the machine he jockeyed at Daytona. "Fireball was a different kind of co-driver than I'd ever had," Grossman told *Automobile Quarterly*. And continued with a story about an incident during Le Mans practice, concerning the fast uphill turn after the pit straight. "If you back off there everyone can hear you," Grossman said. "But it takes a lot of bravery if you're not used to the course." Roberts figured out in a hurry that backing off the gas in that area was not the macho thing to do. "He got a bottle of wine, took a big gulp, went right out and drove straight through there flat-out," Grossman said. The French loved Roberts and chanted "Fie-ah-bool" as he diced over the storied Sarthe circuit. The Grossman and Roberts car had to make two long pit stops, which dropped them down the leaderboard. On the second long stop, the starter failed. "The rules were very strict at Le Mans," Grossman told *Automobile Quarterly*. "We couldn't just replace the starter, we had to rebuild it. It must have taken something like two hours." Jim France told racing journalist D.C. Williams that, "They got as high as third place overall before an alternator broke on the car. Despite it taking them an hour to fix it, they ended up finishing sixth overall." Roberts enjoyed the trip overseas. "Le Mans is a great test of skill," Roberts said after the marathon. "But it takes too doggone long!" News of Roberts' Le Mans exploits received good play in newspapers around the country, further enhancing his image as America's top race car driver.

Much to her chagrin, Judge didn't make that trip overseas. "He said, 'We'll go next time.' This was his first time over there and he wanted to go by himself. He bought me a bottle of Joy perfume. I was frantic with him gone. I didn't know for sure when he was coming home. I was really glad when he came home, but he had a very good time and did very well in the race. He liked that kind of racing."

Roberts touched on the Le Mans experience in the *Sports Illustrated* story:

> "I've done some sports car racing," Fireball says. "I drove in Le Mans in 1962. I liked it. It was very different, particularly the nighttime part of it. We raced at 170 mph with just the headlights – you could only really see far enough ahead of you to react up to speeds of about 70. You had to just talk to yourself and say, 'Well, there isn't anything out there.' I finished sixth overall. You have a co-driver; mine was Bob Grossman. We were battling for second place right up until 22 hours, when we had some mechanical trouble and had to make a pit stop. I didn't really fit into a Ferrari," he added. "I never quite seemed to have enough leg room in there.
>
> "I've never had any desire to be a sports car racer. Stock car racing has been my whole life, and it's grown in popularity and prestige. And the machines aren't that much different. A stock car is a racing machine, just with a stock car body on it. It goes as fast and it corners well. The only difference is stock cars weigh more and so don't stop as well."

Roberts finished the 1962 season with three Grand National wins – all at Daytona, which was quickly overtaking Darlington and the Southern 500 as NASCAR's biggest race – and gaining more and more notoriety.

"He was the first NASCAR superstar and I say 'superstar' because he went to Le Mans and NASCAR used him a lot in other parts of the country, because (stock car racing) was a Southeastern sport," Richard Petty said. "A lot of the other drivers like Curtis Turner, Lee Petty or Junior Johnson, they knew 'em in the South but they didn't know them anywhere else. Fireball was the one driver who leaked out of the South and they were using him (for PR) and he was really good at that."

Historian Greg Fielden agrees: "He was the first nationally known NASCAR racer, well known outside the regional territory of the South. Herb Thomas was one of the great drivers before Fireball's era but he was not known much outside the stompin' grounds. Fireball was featured in a lot of publications that stretched from the Left to Right Coasts."

Bernard Kahn wrote a first-person story for the 1974 Firecracker 400 program that explained first-hand how the name Fireball Roberts had escaped the South and crept into other areas of the country:

> In the late fall of 1961 I was in New York City with Fireball. The evening was chilly and overcast and we were frolicsome and footloose, walking and gawking at the downtown sights. It began to rain just as we passed Roseland, so we ducked into the huge dime a dance entertainment spa.
>
> A hostess seated us up front, took our order for a couple of Scotches, and asked how many dance tickets we wanted to buy. "None," drawled Fireball.
>
> Soon the hostess was back, asking about refilling our drinks. "No thanks, we're still sipping," said Fireball, friendly.
>
> "We'll see about that, I'll get the manager," she snapped.

A few minutes later the hostess came back into sight, with the manager in tow. He was a hulking 260 pound bruiser beautifully equipped to double as bouncer.

"You guys causing trouble?" he said, menacingly. "Get out or I'll throw you out."

"We haven't finished our drinks," said the unabashed Fireball, unblinking.

The muscular manager glared at Fireball, then a look of wonder crept into his eyes and spread over his face. "Say," he said. "Haven't I seen you somewhere? What's your name?"

"Fireball Roberts," replied Fireball, straight faced.

The manager excused himself and said he wanted to get something in his office. A blackjack, I thought. He came trotting down the long aisle shortly, stopped at our table, grabbed a nearby chair and said he was joining us. Looking up at the hostess the manager ordered, "Bring the boys drinks on the house."

He reached under his coat, brought out an 8 x 10 picture and chortled, "I've had this picture of Fireball Roberts up on the wall over my desk for a year. Will you please autograph it for me, Fireball?"

Fireball cheerfully autographed the picture and we wound up as old buddies and lived happily through the night.

Back on the private side of Roberts' life, there was interesting development in 1962. Smokey Yunick took a new bride that year, a young woman named Patty Judge, yes, Judy's kid sister.

In that one-year span Yunick "broke up" with Roberts and married his girlfriend's sister. Huh? If you thought Judge Judge was fuming about

Judy's relationship with Roberts, the teapot really started to whistle when his baby girl married a man 20 years her elder. Judy says Smokey and Patty met on their own and not through the obvious racing link.

"She worked at a dress shop on Seabreeze Boulevard," Judy said. "Smokey, as you know, was a creature of habit. He came across the river every day for lunch at Roger's Restaurant on Seabreeze. Patty went over there to have lunch all the time, too and that's how they met. It was very strange and at the time I was not for that relationship at all because I knew what Smokey was. Glenn kept telling me, 'He's not going to get involved with her.' But they did. He couldn't believe it when they married. My daddy wasn't happy at all. Smokey was what Patty needed at that point. He was older, she needed a daddy, and that's exactly what he was. He told her what to wear, what to cook, everything. He was domineering and she needed that. She had been on her own with me since she was 14. She was thrilled to be married and having children. He was good to her, but he never stopped working. He was driven and never stopped."

Yunick made sporadic Grand National entries through the 1969 season but only saw one more victory, with Indy-car driver Johnny Rutherford in the second Daytona qualifying race in 1963, the year after Roberts won in the big race.

"I got a call from Smokey asking me if I wanted to run a stock car at Daytona and I was flabbergasted because the biggest track I had ever run was a mile dirt," Rutherford said. "The jump to a two-and a-half mile superspeedway was something that this young Texan only dreamed about. I got there and got fitted in the car and we got all signed in and getting close to the first practice session and Smokey said, 'I need to get somebody to answer some questions for you in case you have any. I'll be right back.'

"He came back about 10 minutes later and had two guys in tow with him. He said, 'I want you to meet Joe Weatherly and Fireball Roberts.' Oh man, you could have knocked me over with a feather.

Two of the greatest in stock car racing right there in front of me and they were my tutors for the Daytona 500. 'If you have any questions about going around here, just let these guys know, and they will help you out,' Smokey told me. Fireball said, 'Yeah, it's a little different than what you been running. You need to go out and kind of sneak up on it.' Little Joe says, 'Kid, if your car is right, you can run it flat-footed all the way around here.' That's what I did.

"Fireball was never far away. If I ever had a question, he was very obliging. He was a real gentleman and a helluva racer. He had won the Daytona 500 the year before. I was 24. It was kind of novelty to run a stock car for me. It was a whole different ballgame."

With Yunick's power sedan and driving tips from Roberts, Rutherford became the first driver to win a Grand National race in his first start. "As far as stock car racing, Fireball was at the top, there's no doubt about it," he said. "I felt very fortunate to meet him and race against him. Fireball had an air about him. He knew what he was doing and he knew where he was going and how to get it accomplished."

And Roberts always made time for young drivers, figuring a tip here, some advice there might save him from getting into their mess on the track. When the Pure-Darlington Record Club was established, Roberts was elected president. Why? One of the duties of the office was to instruct rookie drivers about the dangers of superspeedway racing. Darlington PR director Russ Catlin asked a driver, one he knew didn't particularly like Roberts, why he cast a vote for his nemesis for the Record Club office. The driver replied: "We're not stupid. This job calls for teaching rookie drivers and all of us are involved. Fireball is the best teacher of all and will do the best job. You don't have to like him, but you do have to respect him!"

Respect ran wide and deep for Fireball Roberts after the 1962 racing season.

The "Purple People Eater"

If you don't know a damn thing about stock car racing, you need to know this: Fireball Roberts cast the mold for the modern-day driver, and sadly, many of them don't even know it. He did many unique things during his Grand National Series career that are commonplace among today's racing breed.

He was one of the first NASCAR drivers to own and fly his own plane? Why? To keep up with a schedule crammed with personal appearances to make extra money to help settle his divorce. With the airplane he could save a day or two of driving by flying from race to race. Drivers today say they could not survive without a personal aircraft.

Roberts was the only known driver of his era to have a regular workout regimen. He lifted weights to keep his upper body strong to wrestle those beastly stock cars that had no power steering. He also ran on the beach to keep his endurance level high in those marathon 500-mile races.

He was quite concerned about his outward appearance and his presence in public. The drivers he raced against say he was the snappiest dresser on the circuit. And, he worked hard to improve his speech pattern, to use correct English when addressing the media or making a public appearance. "He was a big star and he was just ahead of his time in a lot of things," racing journalist Bob Meyers said.

"Glenn was a big, strong, good-looking guy and could speak pretty well," Max Muhleman said. "His diction was good; you could understand him. He presented himself well. He dressed well. He was clean, clean shaven. He was a very presentable guy in a time when there was an awful lot of Southern guys that had a heavy accent and they were a little hard to understand and they were obtuse in many ways. He was very popular because of the way he looked, and of course, the way he drove."

You can credit Judy Judge for helping transform Fireball Roberts into a public man. "He dressed like they (other racers) dressed when I met him," Judge said. "I wanted his shirt tucked in and not see him in an old white T-shirt. I wanted him to have a button-down collar. If he was going to have a crew cut, then it was going to be a nice crew cut. He was on the right track before I met him. I don't think I would have been attracted to him if he was horribly dressed, but I got rid of a lot of stuff he had and helped him pick out clothes."

And Judge, who was graduated from Stetson University with a teaching degree in 1961, worked on his dialogue. "He knew who he was," she said. "He took some direction from me. I changed the way he dressed and I changed the way he spoke. We worked on diction, dialect and delivery."

The night before a race, Roberts would mentally map out his strategy, based on the track, his previous experience and the competitors starting around him. Again, that is common for today's best drivers, who generally have a strategy meeting with the crew chief the night before a race.

Since he came up the ladder as a self-made racer, he knew the workings of a race car inside and out. Smokey Yunick says in his book: "Now 'Balls' wasn't much help on the race car 'hands on,' but he knew quite a bit about the total race car mechanically, so he could give me clues how to make the car handle." Today's drivers say the communication between the driver and crew chief is essential for success.

And, Roberts realized the dollar value of his star power, by lending his name to products and making personal appearances. He was the first driver to market himself to the general public and reaped huge benefits. Roberts was so ahead of his time, that when asked to compare the more contemporary Dale Earnhardt to Roberts, Greg Fielden had this reply: "I've never compared Fireball to anybody. I've compared others to him because he was such an icon."

One of the reasons he got to be an icon was because of his huge racing success. He had good timing. He always seemed to know when the time was right to move to another team. Such was the case in 1963 when he started the season for Banjo Matthews, a continuation of his odd circumstances in 1962, and moved to Holman-Moody Racing. He made five starts in the Matthews Pontiac before hopping to HMR, which was rapidly becoming the top Grand National race team. If you recall, Roberts had wheeled a Ford for this outfit before, when DePaolo ran the team in 1956-57, but when the factories decided to get out, the driver was cast adrift with a couple of one dollar cars.

Treaties be damned, Ford returned to racing in '63, and by that time, Holman-Moody was spitting out race cars like jelly beans at a candy factory. The team had so much clout that Roberts was able to carry his famed "22" competition number with him even though he was racing for a different manufacturer and Grand National had run a dozen races that season.

Roberts made his Holman-Moody debut on March 31 at Bristol International Speedway and won the race from the third starting position, besting his new, young teammate Fred Lorenzen by five seconds. He added three more wins as the season progressed, including quality victories in the newly lengthened Firecracker 400 at Daytona and the prestigious Southern 500 at Darlington, which Russ Catlin, a PR genius, described as "the perfect race" because there were no caution periods. Roberts' margin of victory was 17 seconds over Panch with Lorenzen grinding his teeth in third place.

After the race, Roberts decided he wanted to go to the resort town of Myrtle Beach, South Carolina, for some down time. It takes about two hours to drive to the beach from Darlington but Roberts wanted to get there in a hurry. "We were driving along the highway at night," Judge said. "A state patrolman stopped us. I don't know how fast Glenn was going. The patrolman came up to the window and said, 'Who do the hell you think you are? Fireball Roberts?' And Glenn said, 'Yes sir.' The next thing I knew Glenn and the trooper had the hood up on our car, looking at the motor of our car. After giving him an autograph, the trooper said 'Have a nice trip Fireball' and off we went."

All went well that first year back at Holman-Moody, despite driving a lavender car. The Ford with the purple hue was apparently the idea of Jacques Passino, who ran Ford's racing program. After wheeling Yunick's masculine black and gold Pontiac, Roberts didn't appreciate his new color scheme.

"Jacques said he wanted everybody to see him coming," Judge said. "He thought Glenn was cocky. I think Jacques didn't like him. I think that was his dig at Glenn. Glenn had a very good contract with Ford. I think Jacques wanted to make a statement with that purple car. Glenn didn't like it but he said, 'As long as it is out front, I don't care.' He knew he wasn't going to be there long."

Roberts got his share of victories in '63, including two superspeedway majors, but 1964 would be a far different story. It started badly when the great Fireball started a very un-Fireball-like 15th and finished 37th in the Daytona 500. The race was captured by the up-and-coming Richard Petty, whose father Lee won the inaugural 500 in 1959. Petty would continue forward to earn championship honors in a factory-backed Plymouth.

Roberts had his own problems. Back with Holman-Moody for a second year of service, he was quietly planning his retirement from driving later that season. He was talking to Falstaff Beer about a very lucrative personal services contract while trying to rid himself of Doris and paying two mortgages. Yes, two house payments. With the extra money he was making on side deals, such as appearances, Roberts was able to buy a house for Judy and himself in 1963. They had grown out of and shed that little apartment Judy had rented since 1959.

The divorce was working its way through the court system in St. Johns County and Roberts was preparing for the horizon, beginning the nesting process with the future Mrs. Glenn Roberts. Because of the ongoing divorce situation, he bought the house on Zelda in his own name, which would prove to have damning consequences. "The realtor was our friend and he begged Glenn to put the house in my name," Judge said. "Glenn said, 'Nope. As soon as the divorce is final. I can't do it now.' We were gone all the time and didn't get it done."

Roberts' divorce was approved and finalized in April, 1964. Roberts and Judge got the news at North Wilkesboro, North Carolina, where he was preparing to race in the Gwyn Staley Memorial 250. Finally free of Doris, several of Roberts' racing friends urged him to marry Judge that weekend.

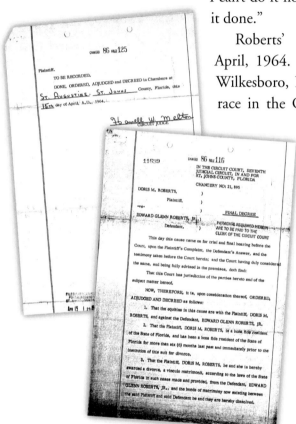

"Gene White and all of them, said 'Let's go get married right now. Let's go get you two married right now," Judge said. "And I said, 'No.' I should have done it, but I couldn't." Roberts wanted a regular wedding with both families present. Both Roberts and Judge wanted to mend all the family fences back in Daytona. She had never met Roberts' parents and she was still on the outs with her father.

"We came back to Daytona and the first night we were back, he took me to his parents' house and, of course, they knew about me but we hadn't been formally introduced. His mother was not very nice, at all, his father was nice, but his mother was not. We got up to leave and she said, 'Where are you going?' Glenn said, 'She's with me.' He said that this is the only time he's ever loved anybody, and if they could not be nice to me then 'You lose me, too.' Glenn's mother then asked us to stay and things would be OK after that. She knew his personality, and she knew that he meant what he said. He could cut you out, when he cut somebody out, they were gone.

"The next night we went to my father's house and daddy was not very nice either, but after they talked, he seemed better with it. We gave him a substantial amount of cash, well, back then it was a lot of money. Glenn asked him to put it in a safety deposit box, for both us of, in case something happened to us in the airplane. If we crashed in the airplane then daddy would have the funds to get us home. Both of us thought that if anything happened to us, it would be in that airplane. Daddy seemed OK with the whole thing and seemed that he understood. He said sorry it happened the way it did, but he believed everything was going to turn out all right."

In a strange twist of fortune, Roberts' private life was now back on course, while his racing career was out of whack. After winning the second race of the 1964 Grand National season, a 417-mile road course race at Augusta (Ga.) International Speedway, he went into a career funk. Yes, he was planning to retire, but if he was going to drive that damned "purple people eater," he wanted to have some victories to show for his effort.

His frustration grew worse as he watched his 29-year-old teammate Lorenzen win five consecutive races, including the spring events at Atlanta and Darlington. Those were the races Fireball was used to winning. "Lorenzen was entrenched as the No. 1 Ford guy," Max Muhleman said. "That was a situation ripe for the drivers to ask, 'Who is getting the best equipment?' Fireball was probably asking that question. I could see it was a difficult thing."

"Glenn thought Freddie was a talented kid but there was a time when Glenn thought Freddie was getting better equipment out of Holman-Moody and he was really ticked about that," Judge said. "He thought their engines were not equal. He let me broach that to John Holman. Holman told me that was just not true. I think Freddie's crew had been together longer, and he lived in Charlotte and was at the shop more. Glenn was not happy with that situation."

"What Holman-Moody wanted to do was win races," Chris Economaki says. "They weren't looking for personality or anything like that."

Dick Thompson, the longtime public relations man at Martinsville (Va.) Speedway, wrote in the 1974 Firecracker 400 race program of the tension and budding rivalry between Roberts and upstart Lorenzen during the 1962 season, before they were teammates:

> Fred Lorenzen, the heir apparent to Fireball's throne, took on Roberts in a race that I'll never forget.
>
> Roberts bolted into the lead immediately, but Lorenzen apparently with a little faster car, stayed on his bumper and tried every way in the world to get around him. Every time Roberts would back off in the turns, Lorenzen would hit his bumper and the crowd went wild.
>
> It sounded like the anvil chorus through the first 102 laps until suddenly, Roberts pulled into the pits with handling problems after an especially loud crunch.

Lorenzen took the lead and his followers roared their approval, but their cheers turned into groans when Freddie pulled into the pits three laps later with a crushed radiator.

Nelson Stacy won the race that day, but there were a many fans surrounding Roberts. "I'm not mad but it was a foolish thing to do," Fireball said. "I was minding my own business when he started bumping. I was running as fast as I wanted to go and if he wanted to pass, he could. I just locked up my brakes and busted his radiator.

"I guess all we proved is that the back end of a Pontiac is tougher than the front end of a Ford."

There was another situation Roberts' wasn't too happy about either. Judy became close friends with "Fast Freddie" after Roberts joined the Holman-Moody operation.

"I had a relationship with Freddie, one that Glenn never had with a woman in his life," Judge said. "Freddie and I were friends, nothing more than friends. I don't think Glenn ever had a relationship with a woman as 'just friends.' He didn't understand that. Freddie was a lost soul, I thought. He was cute, young, and brash and talked like a machine gun. Nobody liked him. I did.

"He was a Northerner from Illinois and he talked like a Yankee from Chicago. And he was winning a lot of races. He adored Glenn Roberts. He was his hero. Anytime Freddie was in town, and Glenn was out to dinner with Doris, Freddie took me out to dinner. Glenn hated that. Any time there was a function I couldn't go to because Glenn had to take Doris, Freddie took me. Glenn hated that. Freddie and I never held hands, kissed, or any of that. We were just friends."

The Wednesday before the 1964 World 600, Roberts took Judge to Young Ford in Charlotte. The Mustang had just been introduced and Roberts bought Judge a candy apple red convertible. "We were supposed to pick it up on Monday, the day after the race," Judge said. "As we were driving away from Young Ford, he told me, 'Go up to Freddie and tell him your engagement ring is big enough for you to sit on. I'm surrounding you with a red Mustang, and that's gonna be your engagement ring.' I looked at him and said, 'Freddie would know that diamonds would mean a whole lot more than any car.' Glenn said, 'Then I gotta get you a five-carat diamond.' I said, 'That *and* a car, and I'll be happy.' "

Judge never got the diamond ring or took delivery of the engagement car. She got nothing.

1962

19 Starts, 9 Poles
12 Races Led
4,312 Laps, 96 Laps Led
3 Wins, Rank: 8
Winnings: $66,152

Dear Diary...

Sunday, May 24

> *It finally happened. The most tragic of all. My darling Glenn was critically burned in a wreck today. I think I'm in shock...I was with Glenn in the emergency room and in his room...We must all pray and none of us can hold our own feelings high. Glenn is all that matters. It is a very long night. My darling Glenn. Please fight. We have so much to live for. Dear heaven, he's such a good man. Let him please get well.*

Those were the first words Judy Judge scribbled in a day-by day diary she kept after her fiancé suffered critical burns following the wreck in the World 600 at Charlotte Motor Speedway. Judge made one entry each day as she staged her vigil at Memorial Hospital. *NASCAR Winston Cup Scene* (Aug. 3, 2000) is the only publication to ever publish the excerpts.

"I never thought he was going to die," she says now. "The doctors, each day, they would say, 'He's a miracle. He's doing well.' I kept thinking he was going to survive. The doctors told me this was not like a gunshot wound to his gut. This was something that would take years to heal; that the scars would have to soften before they could do plastic surgery and all that. 'That's OK,' I would say, 'He can do it. He can handle it.' "

"And that's why I kept the diary. I wanted him to know what was going on all along. I tried to keep it as full as what the doctors said and what was happening so he could have a day-by-day (account). I never thought he was going to die. I thought it was going to be a long haul."

Monday, May 25

Still no encouragement. I did see him today. He asked me who won the race and what really happened to him. His entire body is burned although his face doesn't look too bad to me. Glenn's legs are burned very badly. They say the first critical period is 48 hours. If he comes through this, he might have a chance, but I don't think they think he'll make it. He is so strong-bodied and -willed I know he will – he's got to. God will help him. I know. Bless his heart. I wish it were me. I can't stand to see him hurt so, ...

"The doctors told me, 'He's terribly burned on his legs and back.' They told me they didn't know what they could do," Judge said. "They were calling in specialists from all over the country. They had talked to Ford Motor Company and Ford said they would pay all the bills. They told me, 'We're going to do the best we can.' The next time I came out of the room, his mother and father were there. I think it was like midnight. I'm not sure. Doris came the next day with Pam. By then, they were telling me if Glenn lived 12 more hours, they would feel better; if he lived 24 hours, he would get better. He kept living. At some time in there, Doris went into the room and she was in there five minutes. Glenn's sister JoAnne Roberts went in with her. JoAnne came back out and said, 'You've got to go in there.' He was hysterical. He thought Doris had done something terrible to me. He told everybody he did not want her back in that room. He did not want to see her. Every time she would go in, he would get out of control. She went in very seldom after that and only where he couldn't see her. Sometime during that first week, they said, 'Only the people he called for could go in.' That was fine with me, because I'm the only one he called for. But his mother, father and JoAnne went with me. Sometimes he was lucid and sometimes he wasn't. They told me he wasn't in a lot of pain (in his legs) because all the nerve endings had been burned off."

Tuesday, May 26

I saw Glenn for a few minutes. He asked about the race and said his hands hurt...I can't stop crying. I'm so scared and alone...

In the days after the race, Judge checked out of the Heart of Charlotte motel and moved to a motel closer to the hospital. It was a tough day because most everybody she knew in NASCAR's traveling circus had checked out of the Heart of Charlotte and moved on to the next stop on the circuit. And, she had to pack up Roberts' clothes and belongings, and transfer them to the new motel. "I got his mother a room there, too," Judge said. "I would take her back to the motel at about 8 at night, she would go to sleep, then I would go back to the hospital. I couldn't sleep if I wasn't at the hospital because I never knew when he was going to call for me, and I had to be there when Glenn called for me."

Wednesday, May 27

Things are about the same. Glenn drank some Coke and asked for me. His face looks better to me... The swelling is almost gone. His kidneys are OK and lungs, too. The doctors sounded a little more encouraged, but not much. They aren't sure he will have his legs ... If only I could help him. God help him live. Please hear my prayers God.

Thursday, May 28

Somehow I can't accept this awful thing. I still think it's a nightmare and I'll wake up in Glenn's arms. This can't be true, not just when we were going to get married! I didn't even see him today. It takes them 20 minutes to turn him and 1 hour, 30 minutes to change his bandages. They do this every two hours, so he doesn't get much time to sleep. I know he's burned badly, but dear heaven, don't let it be over. He's a fighter and he'll surprise even the doctors...

Day after tortuous day, Roberts stayed alive, defying all medical odds. Judge was allowed to stay with Roberts the night of the accident because the doctors never imagined he would survive more than 12 hours. Now there was a flicker of hope he might pull out of it. After four days of treatment, the hospital released a statement that the doctors felt he would survive. Strange thing, but they never told Judge that.

Saturday, May 30

They still haven't said he's going to live...I'll do anything. Please give me strength to do what's right and strength to help Glenn.

Sunday, May 31

Dave MacDonald and Eddie Sachs were killed at Indianapolis... I saw Glenn today. Can't get used to his being so "way out" in his mind. His face looks better, but the doctors still won't give us any hope. They said it's an hour-by-hour proposition. Had breakfast with daddy and talked for a long time.

When Judge was allowed into the Intensive Care Unit, she had to "scrub up," wear a gown and mask. The doctors were attempting to keep the area as sterile as possible. She never knew what to expect when she saw Roberts. Sometimes, he was almost normal in conversation. Other times, he was confused or sleeping. It was a round-the-clock effort by the hospital's team of nurses and doctors of continuous treatment and care.

Tuesday, June 2

Glenn is the same as he was yesterday. He might have been a little more active and talkative, but not much. (The doctors) said he was going to surgery tomorrow...he's getting so thin...The doctors don't give us much hope at all. I know he'll make it. Please, Jesus, help Glenn...

Wednesday, June 3

Today Glenn asked me if I was OK. Can you imagine that? He was worried about me! I have no idea of the pain and terror he's going through. I know it must be unbearable. I still would change places with him right now. Why, if this had to happen, didn't it happen to both of us in the airplane?

Friday, June 5

Glenn is delirious and restless...Today he wanted me to tell him "What's going on?" And he said he "was awful sick." His face looks good, but his left side looks awful. He is in a great deal of pain. The doctors say he's doing as well as can be expected, but no one will tell me that he's going to live. In my heart, I know he's going to make it and he will. He may not ever be Fireball again – but Glenn will always be there for me to spend the rest of my life taking care of and loving...

Two weeks after the accident, Judge finally got a positive sign, but it didn't come from the doctors, who had insisted all along the fire had blinded Roberts. "I think I was with JoAnne," Judge said. "We were standing on the sidewalk outside the hospital, outside of Glenn's room. I knew which room was his because I could see the top of his head through the window. I had not seen him for a day. I just stood there so I could see his head. All of a sudden, his big arm goes up and it's flaying all around, and I'm jumping up and down, screaming, 'I love you! I'm here! I love you!' Soon after that, an orderly came flying out of the hospital and said, 'You better get up there or he's coming down here to get you. He has seen you and he's coming to get you.' I went up there and told the doctor, 'You see. He's not blind. He saw me from the fourth floor.' When I got up there, Glenn wanted to know where the hell I had been."

Three days later Roberts' condition had improved to the point where he was moved from intensive care to a private room, which lifted Judge's spirits to no end.

Wednesday, June 10

Glenn was moved from intensive care today. (The doctor) said Glenn was better than he ever had been! I can't say how good that made me feel. Tonight he was very tired but he still was making more sense than usual. For the first time today when I told him I loved him, he told me he loved me, too. It sounded so good to hear those words...

Since Judge was Roberts' only regular visitor, she had seen most of his extensive injuries, which were, to say the least, repulsive. "You're there so long and you see so much," she said. "I got to the point where I would go straight to his face because his face wasn't burned. That way, I didn't have to look at what was there. After the first time they took him to surgery and took (the dead skin off his back) and butt and back of his legs, he was on his tummy and they had a tea towel over his butt. I squatted down to talk to him. The doctor came in, the burn specialist. He said, 'Judy come over here. I want to show you something' and lifted the towel up and Glenn's fanny looked like a roast. There was about a three inch strip of skin that went across his (buttocks), must have been his seatbelt, that wasn't burned. The doctor stuck a probe in there and pulled up something. The doctor said, 'See that? That's perfect. That's the way it has to be before we can get skin back on him.' I just slid down on the floor. I couldn't stand up. My legs wouldn't support me. I don't think I needed to see that. I don't think Glenn ever knew how seriously he was hurt. I know he knew he was hurt, but I don't think he knew the extent of it."

After being moved to a private room, Roberts had more visitors, including his parents. He was fighting infection and a fever, and Judge said he would say things that would hurt feelings. Judge had a full grasp of the situation, Roberts' state of mind, but others didn't, particularly his mother. "One time his mother and I were in there and he said, 'Das,' that's what he called his mother. He said, 'Das, why don't you leave us alone. I just need to hold her (Judge) for a few minutes. Just go away and leave us alone.' His mother started crying, and I felt terrible. But I couldn't stop him from talking. Then he asked me why I didn't take him home, that they were trying to kill him like a mad dog. 'I thought you loved me. If you loved me, you'd take me home,' he told me."

That's when tension escalated between the Roberts family and the Judge kin. Mrs. Roberts, Glenn's mother, told Judge she would have to leave the hospital. "She said I couldn't stay there and if I left, I couldn't go back to the house, our house in Daytona Beach. She said our house was Glenn's house. I called daddy and he was on the next plane and he called a meeting with the doctors and explained the situation to them. He told me, 'You go in there, or I'll do it, and you tell those people that legally, you are in charge. North Carolina is a common-law state and so is Florida. You are his common-law wife. You are registered here as

Mr. and Mrs. Roberts. You are in charge. If anybody leaves, it's going to be them. Legally, you are as married to him as if you were married by the Pope at a high noon mass.' Then he handed the doctor a letter from some judge he knew in North Carolina and it said exactly what he had just told me.

"The doctors told my daddy, 'Mr. Judge, she's the only thing keeping him alive right now. I don't care who she is, she's not going anywhere. It makes no difference to us. They are not going to tell her to do anything.' Daddy felt I was in pretty good standing with the doctors after that. I never said a word to his mother and father after that at the hospital other than, 'I'm not going.' That was all Doris' doing because they told me so later."

Sunday, June 14

Tonight is better. I talked to (a doctor) for a long time. He said, "I am the doctor on this case and I say 90 days until he's released." That sounds much better than six months. He said Glenn was the best burn patient he had ever had – "no burn hysteria"...(The doctor) said it would be at least a year of therapy and exercise until they could graft. The scars have to soften and mature before they can work on them again. Thank, God. Thank, God. Dear God, thank you...

Monday, June 15

The same today. Glenn is still delirious and saying all those wild things. I don't think he knows who I am some of the time. (The doctor) said he had lost at least 25 pounds and would lose one pound per day until he started rebuilding himself. That won't start until they put some skin on him. They shaved his face today and it looks wonderful...

Tuesday, June 16

(They) told us that Glenn had slipped backwards a little on his back. He also said that he is showing some signs of gauntness and malnutrition. He said that (Glenn) would look like a victim of a concentration camp before it's over...He did recognize me today. He is still delirious and semi-conscious...

At this point, the doctors were considering amputation of Roberts' left hand or fingers and one or both of his legs.

Wednesday, June 17

He went to the whirlpool again and his face looks good. They are definitely going to take him to surgery Friday to work on his hand and legs. (The doctor) said his left hand was bad; he couldn't say about his legs yet. The doctors are still saying it's a miracle he's alive. It seems like such along, long time...

After a week of gains, Roberts' condition began to slowly deteriorate. By June 18 he had lost 30 pounds. Each day Roberts would get a whirlpool treatment to clean and soften his wounds. The doctors told Judge on June 21 that they thought Roberts would survive, and they were keeping a close eye on his left hand and leg. The team of doctors started again to talk about Roberts entering another crucial period of recovery. Meanwhile, Roberts' state of mind was beginning to slip.

Tuesday, June 23

Glenn went into surgery at 12:10 today. In recovery room at 4: 30. They found quite a bit of infection and pus on his legs...They completely stripped his legs and left side (of skin). (The doctor) said this week is crucial and he would say that he had a good chance if he made it till Sunday. He also said he was a superior man to have made it this far. He amazes them all. He said Glenn was a living miracle...

Wednesday, June 24

Glenn in the whirlpool today to keep fever down...God, I am so alone now, more than I ever have been. Glenn doesn't know anyone today...He looks worse than he ever has to me...

Thursday, June 25

Glenn does not look good to me today or tonight...He's still delirious and his fever is up...He's going back into surgery tomorrow at 11 a.m. Bless his heart. How much can one human take?...

Friday, June 26

Surgery today, 10:25-6:15. Glenn is very, very sick. (The doctor) said he was "pretty low." I'm so scared. After all this time – 4 weeks and 5 days. He can't give up...

Sunday, June 28

Glenn is much, much worse today. (They) say he is dehydrated. They hope it is not the infection they feared. They are giving him more fluids intravenously and trying to bring his fever down...

Monday, June 29

No better today...His fever had been 103-4 for 76 hours and he had the big infection. They said all they can do is pump the fluids to him and hope his body takes it up. They said the next 12 hours are critical. He doesn't know any of us and is unconscious...

What Judy remembers about Fireball 40 years after his passing

He liked his tomatoes peeled

He gritted his teeth when he slept

He took an aspirin every night before he went to sleep

He had beautiful, big hands…but had cut a tendon on one finger, as a child, and it was bent

He had no chest hair…maybe 4 or 5

He had a flat place on the back of his head

He hd broad shoulders and a cute butt, long skinny legs

He loved his motorcycle and his airplane

He was an excellent pilot and careful every time…and yes, we joined the mile high club

He made up funny limericks

He thought he had a system at Jai Alai…we went a lot, and he learned to play

He was an excellent shot with the shotgun…a triple shooter…three ducks

He was the shuffleboard game champion at our local hangout…he played people with his feet, he was so good…"The Nineteenth Hole"

He shot pool and was an excellent player…great hand, eye coordination

He drank Dewars White Label and vodka tonics, sometimes beer in the summer

He smoked Winstons

He had blue eyes

He was never loud

He was a good dancer and loved to dance

He loved his dog…really, all dogs

He wore a watch and sometimes his Darlington ring, but mostly no jewelry. He won several Rolex watches, but would not wear them because they were too heavy.

He was a great joke teller.

He did not like drunks

He did not do well with stupid questions

He thought the early astronauts were vile, foul mouthed, short men… but brave…we knew them

He never drank the night before a race…and before a 500 mile race, he stopped drinking for a week

He was very protective of his sister, JoAnne

He nicknamed his dear friend, Robert Laney, "Shamus"

He called me "Honey" or "Little One"

He never had to set an alarm, he could wake up when he told himself to wake up

He worked out almost every day

He loved to walk on the beach and did it almost every day when we were home

He did not mind being just with us…he was comfortable alone

I never saw him out of control in public

When he was angry or concentrating, his neck disappeared and his head sat on his shoulders

He was a very careful, slow driver on the street…he told me I drove too fast

He could talk to anyone, from anywhere

He had big dimples on his cheeks

He appreciated and read good books

He liked all kinds of music and sang along to most songs

He wore Old Spice

He used an electric razor

He sucked in when he whistled

He had a crew cut

He thought it was unmanly to cry in public, but he cried in private

He was confident and sure of himself

He walked royally, with long strides

He ate steak cooked medium

His smile lit up a room

He was tall…6ft 2in

He had a gentle soul that he kept extremely private

He thought about things and answered questions or gave directions in very few words

He commanded whatever room he was in

He laughted heartily and from his gut

His eyes lit up when he looked at me

In God's Hands...

On July 1, 1964 one of the doctors leading the fight to save Fireball Roberts asked Judge and Glenn's mother to meet him in a waiting room. "Glenn's mother and I were sitting on the couch and the doctor sat on the coffee table in front of us," said Judge, as her eyes began to fill with tears, 40 years later. "He said Glenn was in 'extremis something,' some kind of medical term. I asked him, 'What does that mean?' He said, 'That means, he's dying.' He looked up at me and tears were rolling down his face. And I hit him. He grabbed my hand and said, 'I'm so sorry. He's going and there's nothing we can do.' "

Edward Glenn Roberts, Jr. was dying of blood poisoning and pneumonia. The infection from his burn injuries had traveled into his bloodstream and worked its way into his lungs. He was having so much trouble breathing, the doctors ordered a tracheotomy. It was now in God's hands. Judge and Roberts' parents spent the last several hours in the room with him as life began to drain from his body.

"Glenn was on a ventilator," Judge said. "They kept sticking a tube in his mouth to clear his throat. He would clamp his teeth down on the tube. The nurse came over to us and she said Glenn couldn't hear anything at that point, but I knew he could hear me when he clamped his teeth down on the tube. I leaned over and said 'Glenn, open your mouth.' And he opened his mouth. I knew he could hear me, so I told him, 'I love you and I will always love you.' And then, he just stopped breathing."

Judge made one last entry into her daily journal at Memorial Hospital (note the date):

Thursday, July 2

  ...There is no life. There is no way to go on living...Our life is over...Love died this morning at 7:12...No tomorrow.

Death Of Roberts Stuns Racing

By The News Staff

The death of Glenn (Fireball) Roberts hung a pall of sadn... tern... whe... with... wer... in... da...

ris Friel, technical director for NASCAR, from Daytona.

Roberts, who numbered three of the July 4 Daytona...

said Marvin Panch, a top driver who was once Roberts' stablemate on the Ford factory team. "I ran with him for a long time and I know.

ic), Curtis Turner (retired from racing) and Fireball.

"No, I'm the only one left racing.

"This is pretty rough on everybody, although most of us ... expected it after we...

Eddie Sachs and Dave Mac Donald were killed on Memorial Day, said, "I didn't know him at two or three races. But I know he was a great race driver, a real good one.

"I was hoping he woul... ... he wa...

'FIREBALL' ROBERTS DIES AFTER 5-WEEK STRUGGLE

Fireball Roberts
Dies July 2nd.

Blood Infec...
Kills Fir...

CHARLOTTE (AP) — Famed stock car driver Glenn (Fireball) Roberts; died today from complications of critical burns he received in a three-car crash during the May 24 World 600-mile race here.

Death came to the 33-year-old Daytona Beach, Fla., driver at 7:15 a.m. at Memorial Hospital.

Doctors listed the causes of death as pneumonia and septicemia (blood poisoning), secondary to burns over 75 per cent of his body, 40 to 45 per cent third degree.

At Roberts' bedside when death came were his mother and father, Mr. and Mrs. Glenn Roberts Sr., his brother, Tommy Roberts, and his 13-year-old daughter, Pamela Jane, all of Daytona Beach.

Roberts, biggest career money winner in the history of the National Association for Stock Car Auto Racing (NASCAR), had been a patient at the hospital since the fiery crash May 24.

His condition had improved until Tuesday when he developed pneumonia and the blood infection. He lapsed into a coma early Wednesday and doctors performed a tracheotomy to aid his breathing. He ran a high fever and received oxygen oft...

NASCAR all 14 So... Darlington 1958 and... Robert... fied car... tered the... to study... ing. He... er 3½ ... ... He... "Fireba... ball pit...

Robe... serious... ing cai... lished... hardes... Grand... His... molish... table... only i...

The... en i... crash... summ... won... at a... ing...

... For... dro... fro... why... ing...

Bill Kiser
Tribune Sports Editor

Bill Kiser
Tribune Sports Editor

The death of Fireball Roberts this morning, en... ed the career of one of the most popular race drivers ... the business.

Roberts was a business man in his style of ra... ing, to say the least.

In fact, some people thought he was a stick-in-the mud because he wouldn't take time out to talk to the fans after a race. But even at the track, Roberts was either thinking racing or talking business.

Fireball's death put six top flight drivers out during the 1964 season.

Joe Weatherly was the first to go when he was killed in a crash at Riverside, Calif. The circuit hasn't been the same without Little Joe. All the color and antics that eased some of the tight nerves around the pits is no more.

Next were Eddie Sachs and Dave McDonald, who were killed in a wreck during the Indy 500.

Then the Rookie of the year, Howard White, injured in a spring race following his honors in the Indy 500 and is paralyzed from the shoulders down.

Jim Hurtibuise, one of the most colorful drivers ever to drive at the brickyard, was also burned seriously and chances are good that his career ended.

And only this morning, the hardest charger on the circuit, Junior Johnson announced that if the speeds got any faster, he was through.

The deaths and injuries of these famed drivers may force NASCAR to cut back on the engine horsepower or start paying out more money to the drivers are yelling about.

The latter is what the current crop of drivers are yelling about.

The World 600, for example, grossed over $572,000 and paid out less than $72,000 to the drivers.

At least these men, risking their lives, should have a better payoff than that.

American Legion Post 51 commander John Cline and Athletic Officer Ben Moose said they would like to thank all those who helped out in the 1964 American Legion program.

"We would like to thank all the fans who supported us this year and we are just sorry that we couldn't make the state playoffs," Cline said.

Moose also expressed his thanks to the radio and newspaper coverage that was given the post this year.

Bobby Biggers, who spent his afternoon off fishing at Oakcliff Wednesday, came home with something for the pot.

Biggers caught a 3½-pound bass which the family enjoyed very much.

Race Hero All-Time Winner

By MAX MUHLEMAN
Charlotte News Sports Writer

Fireball Roberts, stock car racing's all-time major race winner, died today at 7:15 a.m. at Memorial Hospital. His condition had deteriorated rapidly since Tuesday, when

FIREBALL ROBERTS

For Fireball Roberts
Funeral Arrangements To Be Completed Today

CHARLOTTE, N.C. (AP) — Funeral arrangements were to be completed today for famed race driver Glenn (Fireball) Roberts, who died Thursday of complications resulting from burns suffered in the World 600 May 24 at Charlotte.

His body was returned to his native Florida Thursday night. Services were expected to be conducted in Daytona Beach where the Fire Cracker 400 will be run Saturday.

Roberts, who battled for his life for six-weeks like he fought for the lead on the race track, died at 7:15 a.m. of pneumonia and blood poisoning, complications of burns over 75 per cent of his body.

He had been at Memorial Hospital since the fiery crash on the backstretch of the seventh lap at the Charlotte Motor Speedway, the only major...

provement until he suddenly developed pneumonia and a blood infection Tuesday. Doctors performed a tracheotomy early Wednesday to aid Roberts' breathing, but his coma deepened although he appeared to rally briefly Wednesday night.

DAYTONA BEACH, Fla. (AP) — "He was the greatest."

That was the accolade heard most along pit row today as Daytona International Speedway prepared to run its Firecracker 400 stock car race—one of the favorite spots on the racing trail of Glenn (Fireball) Roberts.

Roberts, 35, of Daytona died in a Charlotte Hospital early yesterday of complications from burns he received in a three-car pileup there May 24.

He knew all of the hazards of...

Auto Racing and a close personal friend and confidant of Roberts for years.

"But he made racing his life. We will miss him, but the sport will go on just as he would want it to."

Pit row and the garage area at this famed 2½ mile raceway, where Roberts had some of his finest hours, was a beehive of activity as drivers, mechanics and crews made their sleek cars ready for qualifying for Saturday's race.

But there was a pall of gloom over the area.

"I am an optimist," said Freddie Lorenzen of Elmhurst, Ill., Robert's racing teammate. "I thought he would make it. But now I feel awful. Win or lose, this just isn't going to be a good race for any of us."

A Mountain Is Gone

The NASCAR racing tribe was assembled at Daytona International Speedway on July 2 for practice and qualifying runs in preparation for the Fourth of July Firecracker 400. It was business as usual; the show must go on. NASCAR president Bill France Sr. told the media that Roberts knew all the hazards of the sport and, "We will miss him, but the sport will go on just as he would want it to."

Bad news travels fast, but it's at the speed of light in the tight-knit racing family. By noon anyone who carried a wrench, made sponsorship deals, mounted tires, inspected equipment or drove a race car knew that Fireball Roberts was mercifully out of his pain and agony; that his soul had separated from its charred body; the 1963 Firecracker 400 champion would not return to this holy racing place to defend his title. It was all very surreal.

"Fireball was the idol of all the drivers," Ned Jarrett told the *Associated Press* on July 2. "We looked up to him. He was a gentleman and a sportsman, all that a man in our profession should be. We are going to miss him."

The press squeezed a quote out of Smokey Yunick that day, too. "As a driver, Roberts was about as complicated as the cars he raced," Yunick said. "Finishing second or third was of absolutely no interest to him. He always aimed for the front, and that is the mark of a great driver."

A.J. Foyt, who had won the death-marred '64 Indy 500, told the AP, "Racing has lost a good man. Fireball had a lot of will. That's about all I can say. It's a shock."

Roberts' boss, John Holman said the sports world suffered a huge loss the day he died. "We're certainly going to miss him," Holman said. "I think the doctors and the hospital did a magnificent job of trying to get him well again and they apparently just lost out of the odds. I'm sorry he had to go through all the suffering."

Max Muhleman of the *Charlotte News* wrote that day:

"Fireball Roberts, perhaps the most nearly perfect of all stock car drivers, is dead and it is like awakening to find a mountain suddenly gone.

"He was the one to whom it could not happen, so skillful, so strong, so clever and so colorful that it seemed even old age would have a monumental job of removing him from this world."

Years later, Roberts' Holman-Moody teammate Freddie Lorenzen would say the, "spark was gone; the candle was out; the king was dead." And Roberts' future bride wanted to return home. She had said goodbye to her only lover and best friend only moments before he had tasted his last gasp of air.

When the doctor sat Judge down the day before to deliver the worst possible news – Roberts could die at any time – she called Gene White, who was in Daytona preparing for the race, to come get her with his airplane. When the end came, and Judge had done all she could do, White was waiting at the motel to offer his assistance.

"He got there about 8 o'clock in the morning," Judge said. "When I walked in the motel and told him, we cried. We both cried. I told him, 'There's no pretending now. They will hate me forever.' We got on his plane. I had all of Glenn's dirty clothes and some of his mail."

White flew Judge straight from Charlotte to Daytona then drove her to the Yunicks' house, to her sister Patty, who was swollen pregnant with twins. Over the next several hours, Judge decided she could not live on this planet without her soul mate. "I called daddy," Judge said. "He came to me at Patty's and asked, 'Are you going back to your house?' I said, 'I don't know where to go. That's where my clothes are. But they (Glenn's parents) told me I can't go there.' He said, 'Oh, you can go.' He took me over there and they had changed the locks. Daddy kicked the front door open. And we went in. I went to bed in our bedroom. I got out my little gun Glenn had bought me and I was going to kill myself. Patty had come over and she was very pregnant. She had come and seen the shape I was in so she called Dr. Arthur Schwartz. He was my father's close friend and our family doctor. He came to the house. I was in bed with the gun in my right hand. Arthur was sitting on the side of the bed holding my left hand, telling me why I shouldn't kill myself and that he would give me medicine to make me feel better and that Glenn would not want this."

At that very moment, Judge believed the easiest way to ease her anguish was to take her own life, right there in the very place where she had enjoyed so much pleasure with her future husband.

"From the doorway of our bedroom, our

Max Muhleman

A Mountain Is Gone

Fireball Roberts, perhaps the most nearly perfect of all stock car drivers, is dead and it is like awakening to find a mountain suddenly gone.

He was the one to whom it could not happen, so skillful, so strong, so clever and so colorful that it seemed even old age would have a monumental job of removing him from this world.

The record books bulge with his accomplishments. He was the Mickey Mantle, the Johnny Unitas, the Bob Cousy of stock car racing. To thousands from coast to coast, in fact, he was stock car racing itself.

He was greatest where the odds were steepest—at the big ones. No driver ever won more major events, set more records, led more laps or won more money in stock car racing's premiere events.

* * *

—The Measure Of A Driver

HE WAS a master craftsman in one of the world's most dangerous professions, but he brought such talent and class to it that he seemed beyond the risks that others ran.

There are drivers who ran harder although precious few, but raw speed is not the measure of a racing man.

Knowing when and how and how much is the intangible that separates the great from the near great on a track and on asphalt ovals, on dirt, on road courses, in any kind of machinery Fireball Roberts was the one who consistently came up with the right answers most often.

He won races in virtually every kind of American automobile made. Manufacturers sought his services eagerly for test work, for Roberts could tell them things that were happening at speed that no one else seemed able to detect.

* * *

—It Was His Kind Of Fight

IN HIS final race, the one that ended at 7:15 a.m. today, he did not win but he ran far better than the experts predicted.

Yesterday about 2 p.m. doctors did not give him more than six hours. He passed the six hours and then staged an incredible rally, his fever dropping slightly and color returning to his gaunt cheeks.

But it was too much to ask, even of Fireball Roberts. Infection and pneumonia and the ravages of his terrible burns took him at last.

His mother, an awesomely braver person in her own right, said yesterday when told of her son's failing condition, "No matter what happens, it has been a good, courageous fight."

And that is precisely what it was, the only kind of fight Fireball Roberts ever fought.

bedroom, this voice says, 'He's not even in the ground and already we catch you in bed with another man.' I looked up and it was Doris and Glenn's father. Arthur stood up and said, 'I'm Dr. Schwartz and I'm holding her left hand, which is empty, and her right hand has a gun in it. If I was you, I'd be real careful what I said.' Then he eased over and took the gun from me. Glenn's father said, 'We have come to pick out clothes to bury Glenn Jr.' I said, 'You know where the closet is.' And Doris picked them out. This is the same woman who came to our house to pick up Pam not two months before and when I answered the door, she pushed past me and Glenn came running out of the kitchen. He turned her around, walked her out and said, 'This is the first home I have ever had in my life and I do not want you in it ever. Get out!' "

Doris, the woman scorned, and her former father-in-law, picked out a suit, shirt and accessories, which they delivered to the Baggett-McIntosh Funeral Home, which scheduled visitation the evening of July 4, after the race had been staged at the track. The funeral service would be July 5 at First Baptist Church, the largest house of worship in the city.

"They had told me I couldn't go to the funeral," Judge said. "The night before the funeral, Glenn's daddy called and said I could go to the funeral home, by myself, at 9 o'clock. The visiting hours were from 5 to 7 p.m. He said, 'I mean, by yourself, nobody with you, and say goodbye to Glenn Jr. And you can go to the funeral but you can't sit with the family.' I had dinner with Bob Laney's family that night and left there and went to the funeral home. They had a hundred chairs lined up in there. The casket was closed. There were beer cans and things outside, so you know there had been a big crowd outside. You could just tell. The funeral director knew my family and me. He said, 'Judy, I'm so sorry this is happening, but this is the way they want it. I need to tell you a couple of things.' "

The dimly lit room and casket created an eerie atmosphere. The funeral director gave a simple warning. "I'm going to open the casket for you, but we couldn't embalm him. Are you going to be all right by yourself?"

Judge said, " 'I've been by myself a lot here lately, I can handle it.' He opened the casket for me. I put a picture of he and I in his pocket. I put his Darlington ring in another pocket. And I put a letter I had written him over his heart. I told him, 'This is really hard Glenn. This is hard.'

"The next day Gene and all those guys, my racing friends, came and got me and we went to the funeral. I kept saying, 'I can't do this.' Gene told me, 'He loved you because you were a lady and you be a lady now.' Gene's hand was bleeding where my nails were digging into his palm during the service at the church. When we walked out of the church after the service, there was a big crowd out there. I know what Jackie Kennedy went through because I heard, 'There she is. There she is. There she is.' I could hear that going through the crowd when I walked out."

Fireball Roberts' funeral was a national event and most of the racing community, the big names of the day, turned out to say their last goodbyes, which was atypical of a race driver funeral. Race car drivers don't generally attend funerals because that means stepping a little closer to death and the realities of their chosen profession.

Fireball Roberts once told Bernard Kahn, a pioneer in motorsports journalism and sports editor of the *Daytona Beach Morning Journal*, "People seem to think race car drivers have special courage, it's not so." Doris Roberts was no fan of Kahn's, who at Roberts' request, announced the St. Johns County divorce in the local Volusia County newspaper. Judge said Roberts shouted the news of the divorce to Kahn across a crowded Roger's Restaurant, sparking a brisk round of applause from the patrons that morning.

Max Muhleman, who was one of Roberts' best friends and suffering terrible anguish and loss, painted a poignant scene of the funeral service in a *Charlotte News* column:

Max Muhleman

Jarrett's "Something Extra"

ATLANTA — Jazzily coiffed beauty queens, his beaming blonde wife and a squad of overjoyed rubber-coated mechanics pressed about Ned Jarrett's shoulders in Atlanta Raceway's Vivctory Lane and a swarm of screeching photographers poked their lenses in his face.

It was the high water mark of a long racing career for the transplanted Tar Heel who earlier this year left his Newton home to set up residence in Camden, S. C., dwelling place of Bondy Long, the wealthy young man who sponsors his 1964 Ford.

Not even the national championship he won in 1961 could match the excitement of winning Sunday's Dixie 400, for NASCAR's Grand Natioinal pros are measured by their major race victories and until yesterday the 31-year-old Jarrett could not claim a one.

"Did it feel any different riding out there in front today?" someone asked.

Jarrett for a moment ignored the pressing mob about him and replied, "Yes, in a certain way it did. I couldn't help but feel I had a little more working for me today than I ever had before. The good Lord took good care of me."

It was a sincere expression of the depth of feeling that race drivers all too often are suspected of being incapable of knowing. Jarrett is one who has tried as hard to be a gentleman and polished representative of his sport as he has to win races. Before yesterday, the high esteem in which he has been held by his contemporaries and the championship of 1961 were the only rewards he had to show for his efforts.

He won the 400-miler the way race drivers love to win — running so hard down the stretch that no one was able to catch him. It was a particularly significant achievement in that his was the lone surviving factory-backed Ford in the intensely competitive battle which manufacturers wage on the South's big speed plants.

—'I Didn't Save Roberts' Life'

HIS SPEECH about how different it felt, about the "something extra" he sened as he twisted the stiff black steering wheel about Atlanta's steep banks at 140 miles per hour, referred to the role he played in assisting Fireball Roberts from his blazing car in Charlotte May 24th.

He had ignored the raging gasoline inferno to run to Roberts' aid, sustaining minor burns himself as he ripped pieces of flaming uniform off his friend's blistered body.

But if Jarrett distinguished himself as a brave man by leaping to Roberts' aid and if he soared in stature as a driver by winning the Dixie 400, he also took a giant step in another direction on this bountiful weekend.

Just before the race he told newsmen there was something he wished to straighten out. As politely as possible, he explained that he should not be called a hero, that

Inside First Baptist Church, a huge white stucco structure, air conditioned coolness and the sweet aroma of hundreds of flowers swept over them as they entered silently in small clusters.

The sanctuary floor sloped gently down to a spectacular bank of floral color, stretching from wall to wall. In the middle, beneath a lustrous stained glass window and the minister's pulpit lay the flag-covered bronze casket of Fireball Roberts, stock car driver nonpareil.

It was not the family church. They knew there would not be enough room there. It was the largest sanctuary in town, yet still some were forced to stand in the foyer and outside the door.

Of the hundreds who came to pay final respects there were those who knew him best and those who had never been closer than a race track grandstand; beautiful sun-tanned women, the aged retired couples who people every seaside city, tight-lipped youngsters who had ganged him for autographs and of course the racing people.

John Holman and Ralph Moody, whom he drove for at the end, were there, accompanied by Ford Motor Co. executives. So were Jack Sullivan, his chief mechanic in his last race, and Smokey Yunick, Banjo Matthews, Ray Fox and Red Vogt, who had built cars for him in days gone by. There were Junior Johnson, Buck Baker, Nelson Stacy, Rex White, Lee Roy Yarbrough, Paul Goldsmith, Marvin Panch, Ray Nichels, Glen Wood, Fonty Flock,

Jimmy Thompson, Neil Castles, Buddy Baker and many others.

It was July 5th, the height of the season in one Florida's gaudiest resort towns, but Daytona was strangely quiet as four o'clock struck. Pamphlets at the door read, "In loving memory of E. Glenn Roberts Jr. Born January 20, 1929. Died July 2, 1964."

Rev. C. Norman Bennett began to speak: "You are here that we might remember more than a career. You are here to remember a man. There are few who have the gift of stirring the affection even of those who never saw him. This was strong in Glenn Roberts. It was that more than his skill that caused you to come. Because of this affection we pay respect to his memory."

Just before he finished and the silent audience filed past the casket in final farewell, he said, "As Glenn's father said to me only yesterday, 'He's not just ours. He belongs to everybody.' "

Some of racing's bravest men wept unashamedly as they stood outside the church and watched the casket placed in the blue hearse that would give Fireball Roberts his last ride.

Hundreds of cars joined in the procession to the tropical green serenity of Bellevue Memorial Park, little more than a mile from Daytona Speedway where Roberts was a special sort of king.

All along the route townsfolk had gathered to watch. At the cemetery, hundreds were gathered on a hill that overlooked the interment site, watching silently.

The graveside ceremony was brief, ending in a prayer. The broken family was led away. Most of the rest remained in silence, including Fred Lorenzen, Roberts' teammate and heir apparent. He was white-faced, one hand heavily bandaged. He had demanded to be dismissed from a hospital bed, where he was recovering from injuries sustained in a high-speed accident only two days earlier.

As he left, Ralph Moody remembered, "Fireball said once that he would rather be gone than survive a racing accident so badly crippled that he couldn't race again."

The wish had been fulfilled.

"I almost lost my Christianity over it," Bob Laney said of Fireball's burns, suffering and death. "He was burned pretty bad. Had he recovered, I don't know how he would have lived. I guess God figured it was better that he died than to come back and face all the operations and more suffering."

1963

20 Starts, 2 Poles
12 Races Led
4,643 Laps, 692 Laps Led
4 Wins, Rank: 5
Winnings: $73,060

1964

9 Starts, 0 Poles
2 Races Led
1,702 Laps, 17 Laps Led
1 Win, Rank: 27
Winnings: $28,345

There is a world above,
Where parting is unknown,
A whole eternity of love,
Form'd for the good alone;
And faith beholds the
dying here
Translated to that happier
sphere.

James Montgomery

The Lord gave, and the Lord hath taken away, Blessed be the name of the Lord.

In Loving Memory of

E. GLENN ROBERTS, JR.
Born January 20, 1929
Died July 2, 1964

SERVICES
4 p. m. Sunday, July 5, 1964
First Baptist Church
Daytona Beach, Florida

OFFICIATING
Reverend C. Norman Bennett, Jr.
Calvary Baptist Church
Daytona Beach, Florida

CASKET BEARERS
Traffic Division
Daytona Beach Police Department

INTERMENT
Bellevue Memorial Park
Daytona Beach, Florida

*Please Use Lights
Enroute To Cemetery*

A Hard Act to Follow

Fireball Roberts belonged to the heavens but life was a living hell for Judy Judge, who had spent the last five years of her life with the man she loved, alienated from her family, now despised by Glenn's parents. Just days after the funeral, the Roberts family turned off the electricity and water to the house on Zelda that Glenn and Judy had called home for more than a year. Roberts had put the house in his name only because of the impending divorce and was waiting to marry Judge before tying up all his loose ends. Since the house was in Roberts' name, his immediate heir, daughter Pamela, was the benefactor of all his worldly possessions, including his motorcycle, cars, airplane and the contents of his safety deposit box, which was crammed full of cash. When Judge moved out, leaving most of her clothes and furniture in the house, she had a small box of Roberts' personal effects and "the money that Glenn had given daddy."

Judge moved back into the same apartment she and Glenn had called "the pad" for four years, and she started to drink heavily. "That's all I did for a year," she said. Judge Judge wanted his daughter to sue for the estate as Roberts' common-law wife, but she didn't have the strength to carry on the fight. Doris poured salt on Judy's considerable wounds by moving into the house Roberts' had bought for his future bride. "She moved into our house," Judge said. "She lived in *my* house. I couldn't believe she did that…It all went to Pam because she was the heir. Pam lived there for a while after Doris moved to North Carolina. She called me up and I went over there once when she was married."

After Judy stayed drunk for a year, Patty Judge Yunick brought her big sister back to reality by bringing young Trisha over for a visit. "Patty held Trisha up in my face and said, 'You're not taking her, if you are drinking. You are not going anywhere with her.' I told Patty, 'I can't live here anymore.' She and I sat down and Atlanta was the closest big city where I could get to her if she needed me. I used the money Glenn had given to daddy to make the move. I had some friends in Atlanta, called them, got a job and got out of Daytona. It was really hard to do, but I did it.

"Patty made me realize I was in bad shape. When I moved to Atlanta, I quit drinking, cold turkey. I couldn't do it any longer. I was miserable girl in Atlanta for about three years. I guess that was my grieving period, but I didn't know many people, I was away from home, scared to death, no doctors I knew, no nothing. I spent a lot of time going to psychics. I tried to find Glenn everywhere."

Before she left, Glenn's parents made it a point to apologize to Judge for their bad behavior at the hospital and after their son's death. "They said, 'We didn't know the whole story. She (Doris) kept telling us you were going to take everything from Pam,' " Judge said. "I had no intention of doing that. They asked me to forgive them and I said I would; but it's hard to forget." Glenn's younger sister JoAnne, who lives in Daytona Beach, and Judge remain good friends to this day.

Judge spent the next 34 years as an elementary school teacher finding there was life after the death of Roberts. She had a running battle with Doris over her continual use of "the widow of Fireball Roberts.

"There was a collectible show at Atlanta and I saw in the newspaper she was charging for her signature on his postcards as his widow," Judge said. "And that was fraud I thought. She was charging people for something that she wasn't. She wasn't his widow. I figured she said she was doing that to make money for Pam, but Pam wasn't even there. I just didn't think it was right. It bothered me a lot. One article I read, she said, 'I couldn't go back to Charlotte.' She wasn't in Charlotte to begin with. I mean, please. Glenn was honest and open and tried to do things right. I'm sorry she had a bad death. I'm sorry she died because I know for Pam it's hard not to have a mother; but she lived a lie and she spread it.

"Over the past five years, when there were newspaper stories about 'the widow' I told Pam, 'I'm coming after her. It's not true. It's a lie. She can make all the money she wants as his ex-wife, but she's lying.' That's when I started giving interviews and telling the truth. I just didn't think it was fair to Glenn, as hard as he worked to make that divorce palatable for everybody, and gave her everything. For her to lie was just horrible to me. I couldn't stand that.

"I never, ever, I never said anything ugly about Doris to Pam or anybody else," she added. "I said, 'She wasn't his widow.' I tried to take the high road. That's what I tried to do. I never went back to the races."

Roberts had made a lifelong impact on both women's lives. Doris never remarried. Judge never married. Despite all the misery Judge suffered by having a relationship with Edward Glenn "Fireball" Roberts, Jr., she never regretted her decision or actions, and never considered marrying another man.

"He was a hard act to follow," Judge said. "I still think of him and when I do, my tummy gets tingly. I just never wanted anybody else. I dated other men but I never cared about anybody else. Never fell in love again. I loved teaching school. I made really good friends that I'll have until I die. I think of the things Glenn told me every day. Am I sorry I didn't meet somebody else? I don't know. I think he was enough. I was a little, naïve girl from Daytona Beach who had never done anything. With Glenn, I met presidents and astronauts. I flew my own airplane wherever I was going. I went to Las Vegas, Niagara Falls and Mexico. I did things I would never been able to do without him. He was enough. He touched me in a way that I never believed possible."

In Loving Memory of
E. GLENN ROBERTS, JR.
Born January 20, 1929
Died July 2, 1964

SERVICES
4 p. m. Sunday, July 5, 1964
First Baptist Church
Daytona Beach, Florida

OFFICIATING
Reverend C. Norman Bennett, Jr.
Calvary Baptist Church
Daytona Beach, Florida

1950 - 1964
206 Starts, 35 Poles
90 Races Led
37,230 Laps, 5,970 Laps Led
33 Wins, 122 Top 10
Winnings: $325,643

Epilogue

After Fireball Roberts died, many of the days' top drivers soon retired. Junior Johnson (50 wins) and Ned Jarrett (50 wins) exited in 1966 and Fred Lorenzen (26 wins) called it quits for the first time in '67 then tried an unsuccessful comeback three years later.

"I was sick with stomach ulcers, and I was tired of traveling and living out of a suitcase," Lorenzen told *Circle Track* magazine in 1985. "Most of all, the spark was gone; the candle was out; the king was dead. His death had a great influence and impact on me. He was my god and my teammate, and he was the best. He was the big cheese of the South. He was brains and throttle in a league by himself. I always wanted to be better than he was, so he pushed and drove me to excel."

Roberts was one of four drivers to die in NASCAR competition or related activities in 1964. Joe Weatherly was killed at Riverside, Calif. Jimmy Pardue and Billy Wade died in tire testing as Goodyear was in the process of developing inner-liner technology. The inner-liner, a tire within the tire, is used at most NASCAR tracks today and likely saved many lives.

Goodyear also took the lead in developing a rubber bladder for racing fuel cells, so that no other driver would suffer the same fate as Roberts. The rubber lining keeps the fuel contained in the fuel tank and from spreading over an accident scene.

"There was Fireball's accident and a terrible crash at Indianapolis two weeks later that burned two drivers," Humpy Wheeler said. "We had lost one of NASCAR's biggest stars, if not the star, and here we lost two very prominent Indy drivers." Both Firestone and Goodyear began research into fuel cells to contain gas during an accident. Firestone had an engineer that designed a fuel bladder for warplanes used in World War II. Goodyear was working on a similar project for helicopters being flown in Vietnam. Within a year, fuel cells were being utilized in stock cars.

And, there were conspiracy theories surrounding Roberts' death. Bill Gazaway, who raced modifieds against Roberts in the early 1950s and later became a NASCAR official and worked his way up to Winston Cup Series director, said the accident was just that, all an accident.

He was working pit road as a NASCAR official the day Roberts created the fireball at Charlotte Motor Speedway. "I have never seen a race car burned that bad," Gazaway said. "But you have to remember, that thing was full of fuel. It was everywhere."

Gazaway debunked the theory that Holman-Moody Racing was building very fast but unsafe cars. He put the rumor to rest. "I don't ever recall that there was anything wrong. That car just took one heck of a lick in the rear. And being full of fuel, we didn't have fuel cells. We just had old stock gas tanks and we mounted 'em best we could and when you hit one of those things, you'd bust the gas tank."

In the weeks following Roberts' accident, Charlotte Motor Speedway installed swinging guardrails to close the openings along its inside retaining wall. CMS vice president Richard Howard told the *Charlotte News* he wasn't sure it would have even helped in the Roberts scenario. "We want to make this track as safe as possible for the drivers and spectators. And we will do everything we can to assure this safety for the National 400 here in October," adding later, "I don't know whether swinging guardrails would have made any difference, but we're going to install them anyway in hopes that nothing like this will happen again."

As gruesome as was Roberts' death, others fearlessly answered the call to stock car duty, men such as 1983 NASCAR champion Bobby Allison, who survived his own nightmarish crash in 1988.

"Fireball getting burned was a horrible deal, but one of the things that happened to me early in my racing career was I came up on a highway wreck; a head-on collision between a car with a man and woman and a car with two other women and about six kids and it killed 'em all," Allison said. "But everybody (police, medics) got in their cars and drove away from the scene of the accident and it had an effect on me like, uh, there are things about life that I don't like and I hope I avoid and I got to work to do my best to avoid 'em. Danger (in racing) is part of it. I had already been burned once in a race car and I knew that existed. But I had to accept the chance of peril to take the chance at the success that I wanted and so, that's how, I evened it out like that. It was sad and unfortunate that we lost Fireball, but it was a part of life that we don't have control over."

"It's sad when you think about it," Ray Fox said. "You know, he had so many third-degree burns on him. Today, they probably could have handled it, but back then they couldn't."

Doris McConnell Roberts lived in the Daytona Beach area several years following her ex-husband's death. She then moved out of the house that Roberts bought for Judge and back to Kannapolis, North Carolina, and lived with her mother. She died on May 7, 2004 and is survived by her daughter, Pamela, and several grandchildren.

While today's racing stars know little about Roberts, his star power shined through when he was inducted with the inaugural class at the

International Motorsports Hall of Fame in Talladega, Alabama, in 1990. He was one of 20, including Daytona Beach's Smokey Yunick and Bill France Sr., who received the most coveted honor. "I especially felt bad that Fireball and Mickey (Thompson) were not there," Yunick wrote for *Circle Track*. "We spent so much time together and raced so hard together, I sure wished that they could have walked up there to receive their medals. Looking back, it's plain that most of the men inducted into the Hall were self-educated, self-made men."

Before she died, Doris brought an oil portrait of Roberts to Lowe's Motor Speedway president Humpy Wheeler, who had it placed prominently in the track's Speedway Club. It hangs there today with absolutely no identification, yet Wheeler says most Speedway Club patrons know the name of the man inside the frame.

Wheeler was with Roberts in one of the most embarrassing moments of his life, as a driver. "This happened sometime in the early 1960s," Wheeler said. "He was in a Pontiac Bonneville, brand new, at some motel somewhere. We're going out to eat or something. He backs up, full tilt, wide open and dead centers the stump of a telephone post, it was a fat, short post that somebody had put in the ground. It was probably there to keep you from hitting something. Well, after he hits it, I turned to him and said, 'I can say I've been in a wreck with you now.' It tore that car all up to hell. I don't know how he ever explained that to the guys at Pontiac because it was one of those bring 'em back cars."

As with most Fireball Roberts stories, there was a lot of laughter as the story was told.

"There was no bullshit about him," Tim Sullivan said. "There was no end to his nerve. He drove hard all the way, all the way until the end."

Artist Jeanne Barnes visited the Roberts' grave in 1991 and wrote in her 1992 racing calendar: "It was only 6 a.m. on a very cold morning when I stopped at the cemetery in Daytona Beach while on my way to the Daytona International Speedway. As I walked up to the final resting place of Glenn "Fireball" Roberts, I came upon two other people who were standing there in silence. As they turned away, they nodded to me in recognition. Their names are not important even though you would certainly know them. This short visit happened…over 26 years after Fireball's death. That is how this man still affects people to this day."

Afterword

I had the good fortune of racing against Glenn "Fireball" Roberts from the later part of the 1959 NASCAR Grand National season (now NEXTEL Cup) until the tragic accident in May, 1964, which led to his untimely death. I had the misfortune of being involved in that accident. NASCAR gave me a Heroism Award for my efforts in trying to help Fireball from his burning car. I wish I could have done more. It was the darkest day of my career.

This book tells the story of that tragic day which had a profound affect on auto racing. We lost an extraordinary athlete and individual whom in my opinion was the first superstar of NASCAR. The accident opened the eyes of "the powers that be" for much needed safety features in our sport, such as: fuel cells, flame proof uniforms, track safety improvements, in-car fire extinguishers, and more.

I knew Fireball as a race driver, and had a tremendous respect for his God given talents as a race driver. We became friends around the race tracks. I didn't know all the details of his personal life until I read this book.

I must admit I am not much of a reader. In fact, since my school days I had never read any book from cover to cover until Godwin Kelly sent me a proof copy of this book. I just simply would not find the time to read other books. When I started reading this one I didn't stop. As a result I found the time, and finished it in less than two days.

As I read it I had tears in my eyes at times, and had a few good chuckles as well. I certainly learned much more than I ever dreamed about Fireball's personal life, and marveled at the details which had to take a tremendous amount of time and research to get the absolute facts.

Thanks Godwin for putting into words this very important piece of history of our sport commemorating the life and contributions of a very special hero of mine, and of many.

– Ned Jarrett

Bibliography

Holman-Moody: The Legendary Race Team. Tom Cotter and Al Pierce. MBI Publishing Company, 2002.

Best Damn Garage In Town, The World According To Smokey, All Right you Sons-a-Bitches, Let's Have a Race! Smokey Yunick. Carbon Press, 2001

Daytona USA. William Neely. Aztex Corporation, 1979

Forty Years Of Stock Car Racing, Volumes I, II. Greg Fielden. The Galfield Press, 1988

Circle Track Magazine (October 1985). Freddie Lorenzen. "The Elmhurst Express." Petersen Publishing Company.

Circle Track Magazine (December 1990). Smokey Yunick. "Wallbanger." Petersen Publishing Company.

Firecracker 400 Race Program (July 1974). International Speedway Corporation Publishing

Automobile Quarterly (Volume 39, No. 2 1999), L. Spencer Riggs, "Fireball Roberts, NASCAR's Mr. Prime Time"

Vintage Motorsport (January/February 2002) "Hometown Hero"

1992 Stock Car Racing Calendar, Jeanne Barnes

Stock Car Racing Magazine (January 1967) "Russ Catlin's Portrait of a Professional"

Sports Illustrated (February 1964), Barbara Heilman, "A Cool Fireball Named Roberts." Time Corporation

www.fireballroberts.com (2004) "The Fish Carburetor Story," Webmaster Roland Via

NASCAR Nextel Cup Series 2004 Media Guide

www.indianapolismotorspeedway.com

The Stock Car Racing Encyclopedia, edited by Peter Golenbock and Greg Fielden. MacMillan, 1997.

Archive race reports, columns and feature stories from The Daytona Beach News-Journal, Charlotte News, Charlotte Observer, Orlando Sentinel, Atlanta Constitution.

Photo Credits

Note

Many of the photos in this book are from private collections for which there are no records of the source. While we have made every effort to identify the original source of and give proper attribution, in many cases this was not possible. If you are aware of any omissions, please contact the publisher and it will be corrected in future editions.

Index

ABOUT THE AUTHOR

Godwin Kelly has spent most of his life in the Daytona Beach, Florida area but didn't become interested in racing until after he finished his college schooling.

He went to work for the *News-Journal* newspaper in 1977 and covered his first stock car race two years later. His first assignment was a dilly: a report about the fight between Cale Yarborough and the Allison brothers following the 1979 Daytona 500.

"The sport sucked me in on that cold February day," Kelly says.

Kelly has been on the racing beat since 1982 winning several regional and national writing honors along the way, including two Russ Catlin Motorsports Awards and the prestigious Henry McClemore Award, for career achievement.

Kelly makes his home in Palm Coast, just north of the racing city, with his wife Diane. They have three children.

GODWIN KELLY ON THE ORIGIN OF *FIREBALL*

During the summer of 2004, while researching Fireball Roberts for several newspaper stories on the 40th anniversary of his death, I realized no one had ever done a biography on this man. That's when I got excited.

This was like tripping over a rock in the desert, stumbling into a catacomb and finding a lost treasure. Fireball Roberts was an amazing man who lived an extraordinary life.

Four decades after the placement of his tombstone, Fireball's friends, associates and co-workers still show their raw emotions for this man, who was anything but a typical stock car driver of his day.

Mischievous, spirited and fun loving, yet educated, quiet and detached, Fireball was a man living two lives at the same time. I felt compelled, almost duty bound, to fill in the missing blanks about the man and the myth he left behind.

FIREBALL

This is not a racing book. This is the story of an complex and amazing individual who happened to be one of the greatest race car drivers of his time. The glory days of racing serve as the back drop for a stormy love triangle that was the talk of the tiny resort village of Daytona Beach during the late 50's and early '60s

Glenn "Fireball" Roberts was the first modern superstar of stock car racing. He was truly ahead of his time and already a legend in his late 20's. Unfortunately, for the woman he loved and the racing community, his time ran out far too early.

Godwin Kelly became enamored with this story while working on a special feature story for the Daytona Beach News-Journal's coverage of the 2004 July race. During the research, he discovered there was much more to Glenn Roberts than the "Fireball" persona the public saw.

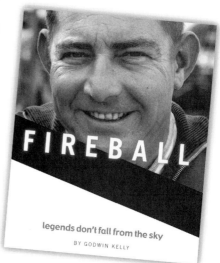

FIREBALL

legends don't fall from the sky
BY GODWIN KELLY

ALSO AVAILABLE FROM CARBON PRESS

Best Damn Garage in Town: The World According to Smokey
   Collector's Edition - $275 (published in 2001)
   Racer's Edition - $95 (published in 2001)
   Pocket Edition - $24.95 (published in 2003)

Sex, Lies & Superspeedways (the audio version of Best Damn Garage in Town)
   Read by John DeLorean, 6 CDs - $29.95 (published in 2002)

MORE Sex, Lies & Superspeedways
   Read by a collection of racing personalities, including Ray Evernham, Dick Berggren, Don Garlits and Dave Bowman, 7 CDs - $29.95 (published in 2003)